JOURNAL
OF A TRAPPER

Nine Years in the Rocky Mountains,
1834–1843

By
OSBORNE RUSSELL

Skyhorse Publishing

Skyhorse Publishing books may be purchased in bulk at special discounts for sales promotion, corporate gifts, fund-raising, or educational purposes. Special editions can also be created to specifications. For details, contact the Special Sales Department, Skyhorse Publishing, 307 West 36th Street, 11th Floor, New York, NY 10018 or info@skyhorsepublishing.com.

Skyhorse® and Skyhorse Publishing® are registered trademarks of Skyhorse Publishing, Inc.®, a Delaware corporation.

www.skyhorsepublishing.com

10 9 8 7 6 5 4 3

Library of Congress Cataloging-in-Publication Data is available on file.

ISBN: 978-1-62087-405-9

Printed in the United States of America

JOURNAL
OF A TRAPPER

TABLE OF CONTENTS

APPENDIX

PREFACE

Reader, if you are in search of the travels of a classical and scientific tourist, please to lay this volume down, and pass on, for this simply informs you what a trapper has seen and experienced. But if you wish to peruse a hunter's rambles among the wild regions of the Rocky Mountains, please to read this, and forgive the author's foibles and imperfections, considering as you pass along that he has been chiefly educated in Nature's school under that rigid tutor, Experience, and you will also bear in mind the author does not hold himself responsible for the correctness of statements made otherwise than from observation.

THE AUTHOR.

PUBLISHER'S NOTE

This edition of *Journal of a Trapper* was originally published in 1921 by SYMS-York Company, Inc. and sold for $5. The editor's notes throughout this text are original to the first publication. The introduction that follows is a note from the original publisher, Lem A. York.

INTRODUCTION

This journal ends so abruptly, with no hint of the personal fortunes of this most interesting author (who, by the way, was a great uncle of the writer of these explanatory notes), that we have gathered such information as we were able from surviving relatives, and append it hereto.

Osborne Russell was born in Maine June 12, 1814. He had very little schooling, and like most of the boys raised on the Kennebec River, dreamed of going to sea. Forbidden by his father to indulge this desire, at the age of sixteen he ran away from home and shipped on a sailing vessel. They had a hard skipper and the crew deserted the vessel when she touched New York. Here he joined the Northwest Fur Trapping & Trading Company, operating principally in Wisconsin and Minnesota. Two or three years in the employ of this company brings the author to the initial chapter of his "Journal," April, 1834. The journal records his fortunes up till June 6, 1843.

From information gathered it appears that Mr. Russell took a prominent part in political affairs, and was a member of the Executive Committee of the Provisional Government of Oregon. The family recollection has it that he was the defeated candidate for Governor of Oregon at the first election under Territorial organization, his defeat being due, in part at least, to his outspoken disapproval of the government's policy in western affairs—notably, refusing military protection to the settlers from the Indians, and at the same time attempting to recruit soldiers from that domain for the war in Mexico.

Hon. John Hailey, pioneer of Oregon and Idaho, who had charge of the Idaho Historical Society exhibit in the Capitol building, has a copy of "Recollections and Opinions of an Old Pioneer," written by Peter H. Burnett, the first governor of the State of California. Judge Burnett was prominent in the political history of Oregon 1843–8, and we find the following mention of Osborne Russell at pages 161–2 of his very interesting book, written about the year of 1860.

"I have already mentioned the name of Judge O. Russell as one of the Rocky Mountain men. He is a native of the State of Maine, and came to the mountains when a young man, in pursuit of health. All his comrades agreed that he never lost his virtuous habits, but always remained true to his principles. He was never married. He was at one time one of the *Executive committee of our Provisional Government in Oregon, and most faithfully did he perform his duty. He is a man of education and of refined feelings. After the discovery of gold he came to the mines, and has been engaged in mining in El Dorado County, California, ever since.

---

* We are informed by Hon. John Hailey that under the Provisional Government of Oregon, the three members of the Executive Committee had practically the same powers and functions as the Governor would have, or in other words, instead of electing a Governor, they elected three men to act in that capacity.—Ed.

When in Oregon he was occasionally a guest at my house, and would for hours together entertain us with descriptions of mountain life and scenery. His descriptive powers were fine, and he would talk till a late hour at night. My whole family were deeply attentive and my children yet remember the Judge with great pleasure. He was always a most welcome guest at my house. He did not tell so many extraordinary stories as the average Rocky Mountain trapper and hunter, but those he did tell were true."

Then followed a description of the encounter with a grizzly, practically as recorded on page 12 of this book.

In 1848 Mr. Russell left Oregon for Sacramento, California, and the gold fields. The following letters, which are in good state of preservation, explains conditions better than we could describe them and we give them verbatim:

Oregon, Polk County, April 4th, 1848.

Dear Sister:

I received the letters from Martha and yourself dated January 31st, '47, on the 18th day of September, last; your own experience will dictate to you the inexpressible delight which I felt on the receipt of them, better than my pen can describe it. A person by the name of Hanford brought these letters from the States to Oregon but I have never been able to see him, or learn anything from your friend Haket. This is the first opportunity I have had of answering your letter; a party is now about to start across the mountains to the States, to which I entrust the care of a letter to yourself and one to Martha Ann.

I cannot answer my brother's letters until I receive them. It would afford me the greatest satisfaction to comply with your earnest request "to come home" and visit with you all, but it is a pleasure which reason dictates that I must forego at present, as my presence in Oregon is indispensably necessary, until the United States extend their jurisdiction over us, in order to acquire title to my lands and property. Nevertheless, I sincerely hope the time is not far distant, when my ardent desires to see my native land will be fulfilled.

It affords me consolation to know that you have a partner suited to your wishes. May your days glide smoothly in uninterrupted happiness and may you continue to dwell in the affections of your husband and favour of your God, and may Lemuel by a faithful discharge of the duties he owes to his family, to society, to his country and his God, continue to merit those affections.

We have had one of the most pleasant winters I ever experienced. The grass has been remarkably fine all winter, and the finest quality of beef is now killed from the natural pastures. Garden vegetables such as beets, onions, turnips, potatoes, and in fact nearly all roots, do the best in this country, to stand in the ground all winter, especially where the soil is inclined to be sandy, as we never have frost sufficient to injure them. The wheat promises an extraordinary crop this year; it is thought it will average twenty-five bushels to the acre throughout the country. It was generally put in the ground in autumn or the early part of winter, although winter wheat can be sown here in any month of the year. You who have never seen what is called a prairie country, can form but a faint idea of the beauty of its scenery. A diversity of oak-covered hills, cleared of underbrush as if by the hand of art, and plains covered with the most luxuriant verdure, intersected with small streams from the mountains, whose serpentine courses divide them into convenient farms, which are supplied with wood and timber from the narrow groves along their banks, or the oak groves on the intervening hills, constitute the face of this valley as viewed from my residence eastward, until the sight is lost in the smoky atmosphere thirty miles distant, or rests on the towering peaks of Mount Washington and Jefferson, with their snow-crowned heads,

> That ofttimes pierce the onward fleeting mists,
> Whose feet are washed by gentle summer showers,
> Whilst Phoebus' rays play on their sparkling crests.

But, my dear sister, beautiful as this country is, that is, this portion of it (for I now speak only of the Willamette valley) my better reason would not prompt me to wish you were here at present, although the contemplation of the scenery around me often dictates the wish that not only you, but all the family were here. We have to undergo, the best of us, in this country, privations of which you are little acquainted, and which must always be expected in the settlement of a new country.

We are now engaged in an expensive Indian war which we have been unavoidably drawn into, but the theatre of action is 200 miles from this valley. The particulars of this war I have briefly described in Martha's letter.

My health is very good in comparison to what it has formerly been.

Give my best respects to your husband, and tell him that although we are not personally acquainted, yet a letter from him would be received as a favour. Give my love to your children and my respects to all inquiring friends.

Write every opportunity.

And now, that the God of heaven may bless you and yours, and his spirit guide you in the path of duty, direct through and protect you from the snares and temptations which the flesh is subject to in this world, and bring you to everlasting happiness, is the sincere prayer of your affectionate brother,

OSBORNE RUSSELL.

———

Oregon, Polk County, April 3, 1848.

Dear Sister:

I received your letter, dated January 31st, '47, on the 18th of September last, and the one dated 16th March on the 1st of October; and if your last letter speaks the language of your heart (which I do not doubt) you can imagine in some degree my feelings upon receipt of letters from the dearest female relations I have on Earth. And when your eyes rest upon the date of this letter, do not impute it to a want of regard or negligence, that an answer to your letters has so long been delayed. In Oregon we are all mere creatures of chance so far at least as regards communication with the civilized world; and indeed, I sometimes fear the "masterly inactivity" of the government of the United States towards affording protection to the people of Oregon will drive them to a desperate extreme.

Congress has treated us with a shameful neglect which we do not deserve.

Notwithstanding our feeble resources, we are now involved in an expensive Indian war, the cause of which I shall briefly relate.

On the 29th of November last, the Cayuse Indians, who live 300 miles up the Columbia, massacred fourteen white persons, most of whom were missionaries residing among them, among whom were Dr. Marcus Whitman and his estimable lady, who had founded the mission among the Cayuses in 1837 under the auspices of the American Board of Boston. The only cause they could assign for the commission of such an atrocious deed was a report secretly spread among them, that Dr. Whitman and the whites wished to kill them and take their lands, and for that purpose, the last immigration from the States had introduced the measles among them. It is true the last immigration did fetch the measles into all the inhabited parts of Oregon, the effects of which have proven severe on the Indians from their mode of treating the disease. There were several families of whites amounting to upwards of seventy persons residing among the Cayuses at the mission. The men were nearly all killed and the women subjected to indignities too horrid to be described, for about twelve days, when their freedom was purchased by the Hudson's Bay Company.

The name of Peter S. Ogden will long be remembered with gratitude, not only by those he so timely released from such a dreadful captivity, but by every American in Oregon who has a heart susceptible of feeling.

Our Legislature being in session at the time the distressing news arrived at Oregon City, measures were immediately adopted for raising and equipping 500 men for the purpose of punishing the Cayuses as their crime deserved.

Whilst seated at the table writing this letter I have received intelligence from the regiment, which started on the campaign in January last. They have had several skirmishes with the Indians and killed sixty of them. The whites have lost four killed and fifteen wounded. The colonel has been killed in camp by an accidental shot from a rifle. The lieutenant colonel has been wounded in the knee. A treaty has been concluded with the neighboring tribes, and the Cayuses have been informed that a treaty of peace will be made with them on no other consideration than delivering up the murderers and paying of the war expenses. And worse than all, the regiment is much in want of ammunition. I said worse than all, but I recall the expression; our worst treatment comes from our mother country who, instead of affording us the protection we have so long prayed for, she has sent a ship to us modestly requesting 500 men to assist in the war with Mexico!

Alas! has it come to this? A colony of American citizens living on American soil, continually imploring protection in the most humiliating manner for nine years, and then meet with such a response as this! It is but too true. Citizens and subjects of foreign governments deride us with the neglect of our government, and what can we say in its defense? With shame and confusion we are subjected to the humiliating confession of the truth. We are informed that Congress at their last session passed an act to establish a mail by sea from the United States to Oregon, but the information of such an act being passed is all the benefit we have as yet derived from it.

But our political circumstance is too gloomy a subject for me to dwell longer upon, even if time and space would permit. And now, my dear sister, since the rehearsal of a few out of the many of our political misfortunes have put me somewhat in an ill humor, I hope to be forgiven if you should feel a little of its effects.

Are you aware that your letter dated January 31st, the first I ever received from you, and which now lays open before me, is not even embellished with your signature, and your name nowhere to be seen on the sheet? Now, I think such a nice, clean, and above all, such an affectionate letter, should not have been ashamed to bear the signature of its fair author, and the only excuse I can frame for the omission was the indisposition of which you complained when you wrote.

I return you an affectionate brother's thanks for the souvenir I received enclosed in your second letter, which although of small nominal value, I assure you is highly esteemed, and would be doubly so had the letters comprising the motto been wrought with your own fair hair.

You seemed to be pleased that I was not married, but I assure you that should I get married in this country, or should death (who is no respecter of persons) overtake me, my last will will testify my regard for you. Your affectionate letters have added much to my anxiety to visit Maine. I have not at present the least inclination to marry in this country. But I must first secure the title to my lands before I can visit the United States.

My health since I wrote last has been better than formerly.

The past winter has been the finest I ever saw; the finest quality of beef is now being killed from the natural pastures. Oregon promises a more abundant crop of wheat this year than was ever before known in this country.

I have sent my journal of mine residence in the Rocky Mountains to New York for publication, and have instructed my agent at that place to forward you a copy of it when published.

Give my best wishes to Daniel, Lemuel, and families, and tell them that I cannot anticipate the contents of their letters enough to answer them before I receive them. Since the year 1834 I have received five letters from my relatives, viz., one from Daniel, one from Samuel, one from Eleanor, and two from yourself.

You thought I had better go to Maine and get a load of Kennebec girls and fetch out to Oregon. Such a cargo would doubtless find a ready market in Oregon, if the policy of insurance upon it were not purchased too dear, and I think no man in his right senses would ship such a cargo without having it insured, not only against the insults of Neptune, but the wantonness of Cupid.

Give my best compliments to Uncle Sam and Ursula, and tell the old gentleman I have known jokes accidentally turned into hard earnest. And tell those who are solicitous about gaining mother's consent on my behalf that it is not impossible that I may appear among them some day like Irving's Dutchman after twenty years' sleep.

Give my respects to old Mr. Boswell and family and all others who feel enough interested to inquire for me.

It is a great consolation to me to think that you live happy and contented. Notwithstanding my philosophy has never taught me how happy three clams can live in a junk bottle, it teaches me that true happiness is contentment, and vice versa.

Give mother the love of an affectionate son and William that of a brother. Tell mother I should be extremely glad to grant her request to "come home," but it is impossible for me to do so at present without a sacrifice which, I dare say, she would not wish me to make; but do not despair of seeing me at no far distant period. I should have been in Hallowell before this, had the United States extended their jurisdiction and gave security to my property.

Another subject occurs to my memory which I had almost forgotten. Before I left Maine, grandfather sent to the family a recipe for making pills; if that recipe is in being I wish to obtain a copy of it, and shall consider it a great favor if you will forward it by the first opportunity.

You half expressed a wish to be with me to enjoy with me the evening hours. Could I harbour a wish that you should leave mother, the next one of all others would be that you were with me. Write every opportunity. If the mail goes into operation this year by way of Panama, we shall have a better opportunity for communication. I write to Eleanor tomorrow in answer to her letter. My time is brief and the sheet full; I will therefore close this epistle by imploring the blessing of that Being in whom we live, move and have our being, now and forever. Adieu from your brother,

OSBORNE RUSSELL.

California (Gold Mines) Nov. 10, 1849.

Dear Sister:—You will not probably be astonished when you see my locality at the date of this letter, as I think Maine, and even Hallowell, must by this time have had a touch of the gold fever.

I left Oregon last September for this country by land, and arrived here on the 25th of the same, and on the 20th of October was attacked with the bilious fever, which lasted until winter. I remained in the mines during the winter and until now, and shall also spend this winter in the mines.

Owing to my ill health last winter I engaged in merchandising; in March commenced collecting gold with my own hands and continued working until the first of October, when I commenced business under the firm of Russell & Gilliam—provision store and boarding house—my partner, an old neighbor from Oregon, having his family here. We are doing a thriving business for this country. About 30,000 people have come across land to this country this season. The old miners, I think average from $12 to $16 per day, estimating gold at $6 per ounce.

Cities and towns are rising up among the hills and mountains in the gold region as if by the effect of magic.

The place where we are located is called Gallowstown. It is situated fifty-five miles east of the city of Sacramento, on the south side, within four miles of the American River. It takes the name from the fact of our having hung three men for murder last winter. Your brother sat as one of the judges pro tempore on the trial. Since that dreadful execution, this has been one of the most quiet communities I ever lived in.

Some people here are getting gold by the pound per day, and others not making more than their board, and I am informed it is the same throughout the mines, which are nearly 400 miles in length—confined entirely to the hills, mountain streams and ravines. The most I have ever dug in a day was $100, but have frequently obtained $40 to $60 per day.

The gold here in this place is coarse, from one-half dollar to six ounces in a piece, yet some is so fine that it can hardly be seen with the naked eye. But let this suffice for the gold diggings and let something else take its place.

I received a letter from Martha, dated September 24th, 1848, in which she informed me that she was to be married in December, and that is the only cause why she does not get an answer from me. Not that I have the least wish to prevent her from uniting with the man of her choice, but I must hear of her being certainly married, and to whom, before I shall know how to direct a letter to her, as this life is filled with uncertainties.

A gentleman from Thomaston, Maine, with whom I became acquainted this spring, stepping into the store today, told me he should start for Maine on the 12th and should pass through Lewiston, as he had some relatives living there. I also having a dear relative living there, determined at once to send her a letter, although she has not yet answered my last.

I am in good health, good spirits, and full of business at present, and it is now near eleven o'clock at night and I must yet write a few lines to Daniel before I sleep. When I shall see Maine I cannot tell, but expect to see it before long and fetch with me some of the California gold. But people value not gold here as they would in the United States. The sight of so much of it makes it familiar to them and depreciates its value. Silver coin seems like iron.

Give my best respects to Mr. Read and an uncle's love to your children, with compliments to all inquiring friends.

Send your letters to Sacramento City, California, by the first opportunity, and believe me to be your most affectionate brother,

OSBORNE RUSSELL.

To his sister Eleanor.

The letter had no envelope, but was folded and sealed with wax, as was customary at that date, and addressed on the back as follows:

Mrs. Eleanor Read,

Lewiston, Maine.

By the politeness of Mr. Kinney.

Mrs. Read was our grandmother. "Martha," to whom he refers, was his younger sister, and Daniel was his cousin.

To continue. It seems that Osborne Russell prospered in his mining and merchandising, and that he and a partner later acquired two vessels which plied between Sacramento and Portland. During one of his trips to the mines, the partner absconded, after collecting all he could of the firm's money, taking a loaded boat to Oregon and also disposing of that. Mr. Russell spent the balance of his days trying to repay their creditors, finally being attacked by what was temed "miner's rheumatism," which paralyzed him from the waist down, and he spent the last year of his eventful life in the county hospital at Placerville, El Dorado County. We have been unable to get the date of his death, but have been informed that he was satisfied to die, and at peace with the world and his Maker.

A limited edition of this "Journal" was published by us in 1914 and distributed to relatives, friends and historical societies. There has later been such an insistent demand for copies of this work that we have printed another edition, adding the "Appendix" which was omitted by us in the former book, and copies may be had from the Publishers.

L. A. YORK.

Boise, Idaho, July 25, 1921.

JOURNAL OF A TRAPPER

CHAPTER I

Expedition Left Independence, Missouri, April 28, 1834, Headed by
Nathaniel J. Wyeth

At the town of Independence, Mo., on the 4th of April,
1834, I joined an expedition fitted out for the Rocky Mountains and mouth of the Columbia River, by a company formed in Boston under the name and style of the Columbia
River Fishing and Trading Company. The same firm had fitted out a brig of two hundred tons burden, freighted with the
necessary assortment of merchandise for the salmon and fur
trade, with orders to sail to the mouth of the Columbia River,
whilst the land party, under the direction of Mr. Nathaniel
J. Wyeth, should proceed across the Rocky Mountains and
unite with the brig's company in establishing a post on the
Columbia near the Pacific.

Our party consisted of forty men engaged in the service,
accompanied by Messrs. Nutall and Townsend, botanists and
ornithologists, with two attendants; likewise Revs. Jason and
Daniel Lee, Methodist missionaries, with four attendants, on
their way to establish a mission in Oregon, which brought our
numbers (including six independent trappers) to fifty-eight
men. From the 23rd to the 27th of April we were engaged in

arranging our packs and moving to a place about four miles from Independence. On the morning of the 28th we were all equipped and mounted hunter-like. About forty men leading two loaded horses each were marched out in double file with joyous hearts, enlivened by anticipated prospects, led by Mr. Wyeth, a persevering adventurer and lover of enterprise, whilst the remainder of the party, with twenty head of extra horses and as many cattle to supply emergencies, brought up the rear under the direction of Captain Joseph Thing, an eminent navigator and fearless son of Neptune, who had been employed by the company in Boston to accompany the party and measure the route across the Rocky Mountains by astronomical observation.

We traveled slowly through the beautiful, verdant and widely extended prairie until about two o'clock PM and encamped at a small grove of timber near a spring. On the 29th we took up our march and traveled across a large and beautifully undulating prairie, intersected by small streams skirted with timber intermingled with shrubbery, until the 3d day of May, when we arrived at the Kaw or Kansas River, near the residence of the United States agent for those Indians.

The Kaw or Kansas Indians are the most filthy, indolent and degraded set of human beings I ever saw. They live in small, oval huts four or five feet high, formed of willow branches and covered with, deer, elk or buffalo skins.

On the 4th of May we crossed the river and on the 5th resumed our march into the interior, traveling over beautiful rolling prairies and encamping on small streams at night until the 10th, when we arrived at the River Platte. We followed up this river to the forks, then forded the south fork and traveled up the north until the 1st day of June, when we arrived at Laramie's Fork of the Platte, where is the first perceptible commencement of the Rocky Mountains. We crossed this fork and traveled up the main river until night and encamped. The next day we left the river and traveled across Black Hills nearly parallel with the general course of the Platte until the 9th of June, when we came to the river again and crossed it at a place called the Red Buttes (high mountains of red rock from which the river issues). The next day we left the river on our left and traveled a northwest direction, and stopped at night on a small spring branch, nearly destitute of wood or shrubbery. The next day we arrived at a stream running into the Platte, called Sweetwater. This we ascended to a rocky, mountainous country until the 15th of June, then left it and crossed the divide between the waters of the Atlantic and Pacific oceans, and encamped on Sandy Creek, a branch running into Green River, which flows into the Colorado of the West. The next day we moved down Sandy west northwest direction and arrived at Green River on the 18th of June. Here we found some white hunters, who informed us that the grand rendezvous of the whites and Indians would be on a small western branch of the river about twenty miles distant, in a Southwest direction. Next day, June 20th, we arrived at the destined place. Here we met with two companies of trappers and traders. One was a branch of the American Fur Company, under the direction of Messrs. Dripps and Fontanell; the other was called the Rocky Mountain Fur Company. The names of the partners were Thomas Fitzpatrick, Milton Sublett, and James Bridger. The two companies consisted of about 600 men, including men engaged in the service, white, halfbreed, and Indian fur trappers. This stream was called Ham's Fork of Green River. The face of the adjacent country was very mountainous and broken, except the small alluvial bottoms along the streams. It abounded with buffalo, antelope, elk, and bear and some few deer along the river. Here Mr. Wyeth disposed of a part of his loads to the Rocky Mountain Fur Company, and on the 2d of July we renewed our march towards the Columbia River. After leaving Ham's Fork we took across a high range of hills in a northwest direction and fell on a stream called Bear River, which emptied into the Big Salt Lake. This was a beautiful country. The river, which was about twenty yards wide, ran through large, fertile bottoms bordered by rolling ridges which gradually ascended on each side of the river to the high ranges of dark and lofty mountains upon whose tops the snow remained nearly the year round. We traveled down this river northwest about fifteen miles and encamped opposite a lake of fresh water about sixty miles in circumference, which outlet into the river on the west side. Along the west border of this lake the country was generally smooth, ascending gradually into the interior and terminating in a high range of mountains which nearly surrounded the lake, approaching close to the shore on the east. The next day, the 7th, we traveled down the river and on the 9th we encamped at a place called the Sheep Rock, so called from a point of the mountain terminating at the river bank in a perpendicular high rock. The river curved around the foot of this rock and formed a half circle, which brought its course to the southwest, from whence it ran in the same direction to the Salt Lake, about eighty miles distant. The sheep occupied this prominent elevation (which overlooked the surrounding country to a great extent) at all seasons of the year.

On the right hand or east side of the river about two miles above the rock were five or six mineral springs, some of which had precisely the taste of soda water when taken up and drank immediately; others had a sour, sulphurous taste; none of them had any outlet, but boiled and bubbled in small holes a few inches from the surface of the ground. This place which looked so lonely, visited only by the rambling trapper or solitary savage, will doubtless at no distant day, be a resort for thousands of the gay and fashionable world, as well as invalids and spectators. The country immediately adjacent seemed to have all undergone volcanic action at some remote period, the evidences of which, however, still remained in the deep and frightful chasms which might be found in the rocks throughout this portion of the country and which could only have been formed by some terrible convulsion of nature. The ground about these springs was very strongly impregnated with salsoda. There were also large beds of clay in the vicinity, of a snowy whiteness, used by the Indians for cleansing their clothes and skins, it not being inferior to any soap for cleansing woolens or skins, dressed after the Indian fashion.

CHAPTER II

Meeting With Captain B.S. Bonneville and Party—Establishment of the Trading Post at Fort Hall

On July 11th we left Bear River and crossed low ridges of broken country for about fifteen miles in a northeast direction, and fell on to a stream which ran into the Snake River, called Blackfoot. Here we met with Captain B.S. Bonneville and a party of ten or twelve men. He was on his way to the Columbia and was employed killing and drying buffalo meat for the journey. The next day we traveled in a westerly direction over a rough, mountainous country about twenty-five miles, and the day following, after traveling about twenty miles in the same direction, we emerged from the mountains into the great valley of the Snake River. On the 16th we crossed the valley and reached the river in about twenty-five miles travel west. Here Mr. Wyeth concluded to stop, build a fort and deposit the remainder of his merchandise, leaving a few men to protect them, and trade with the Snake and Bannock Indians.

On the 18th we commenced the fort, which was a stockade eighty feet square, built of cottonwood trees set on end, sunk two and one-half feet in the ground and standing about fifteen feet above, with two bastions eight feet square at the opposite angles. On the 4th of August the fort was completed and on the 5th the "Stars and Stripes" were unfurled to the breeze at sunrise in the center of a savage and uncivilized country, over an American trading post.

The next day Mr. Wyeth departed for the mouth of the Columbia River with all the party excepting twelve men (myself included) who were stationed at the fort. I now began to experience the difficulties attending a mountaineer, we being all raw hands, excepting the man who had charge of the fort, and a mulatto, the two latter having but very little experience in hunting game with the rifle, and although the country abounded with game, still it wanted experience to kill it.

On the 12th of August myself and three others (the mulatto included) started from the fort to hunt buffalo. We proceeded up the stream running into Snake River near the fort called Ross Fork in an easterly direction about twenty-five miles, crossed a low mountain in the same direction about five miles and fell on to a stream called the Portneuf. Here we found several large bands of buffalo. We went to a small stream and encamped. I now prepared myself for the first time in my life to kill meat for my supper, with a rifle. I had an elegant one, but had little experience in using it. However, I approached the band of buffaloes, crawling on my hands and knees within about eighty yards of them, then raised my body erect, took aim and shot at a bull. At the crack of the gun the buffaloes all ran off excepting the bull which I had wounded. I then reloaded and shot as fast as I could until I had driven twenty-five bullets at, in, and about him, which was all that I had in my bullet pouch, while the the bull still stood, apparently riveted to the spot. I watched him anxiously for half an hour in hopes of seeing him fall, but to no purpose. I was obliged to give it up as a bad job and retreat to our encampment without meat; but the mulatto had better luck—he had killed a fat cow while shooting fifteen bullets at the band. The next day we succeded in killing another cow and two bulls. We butchered them, took the meat and returned to the fort.

Experience With a Grizzly Bear

On the 20th of August we started again to hunt meat. We left the fort and traveled about six miles, when we discovered a grizzly bear digging and eating roots in a piece of marshy ground near a large bunch of willows. The mulatto approached within 100 yards and shot him through the left shoulder. He gave a hideous growl and sprang into the thicket. The mulatto then said: "Let him go; he is a dangerous varmint," but not being acquainted with the nature of these animals I determined on making another trial, and persuaded the mulatto to assist me. We walked around the bunch of willows where the bear lay, keeping close together, with our rifles ready cocked and presented towards the bushes, until near the place where he had entered, when we heard a sullen growl about ten feet from us, which was instantly followed by a spring of the bear toward us, his enormous jaws extended and eyes flashing fire. Oh Heavens! was ever anything so hideous? We could not retain sufficient presence of mind to shoot at him but took to our heels, separating as we ran, the bear taking after me. Finding I could outrun him, he left and turned to the other, who wheeled about and discharged his rifle, covering the bear with smoke and fire, the ball, however, missing him. He turned and bounded toward me. I could go no further without jumping into a large quagmire which hemmed me in on three sides. I was obliged to turn about and face him. He came within about ten paces of me, then suddenly stopped and raised his ponderous body erect, his mouth wide open, gazing at me with a beastly laugh. At this moment I pulled trigger, as I knew not what else to do and hardly knew that I did this, but it accidentally happened that my rifle was pointed towards the bear when I pulled and the ball piercing his heart, he gave one bound from me, uttered a deathly howl and fell dead, but I trembled as if I had an ague fit for half an hour after. We butchered him, as he was very fat, packed the meat and skin on our horses and returned to the fort with the trophies of our bravery, but I secretly determined in my own mind never to molest another wounded grizzly bear in a marsh or thicket.

On the 26th of September, our stock of provisions beginning to get short, four men started again to hunt buffalo. As I had been out several times in succession, I concluded to stay in the fort awhile and let others try it. This was the most lonely and dreary place I think I ever saw—not a human to be seen excepting the men about the fort. The country was very smoky and the weather sultry and hot. On the first day of October our hunters arrived with news which caused some little excitement among us. They had discovered a village of Indians on Blackfoot Creek, about twenty-five miles from the fort in a northeasterly direction, consisting of about sixty lodges. They had ridden, greenhorn-like, into the village without any ceremony or knowledge of the friendly or hostile disposition of the Indians, neither could they inform us to what nation they belonged. It happened, however, that they were Snake, friendly to the whites, and treated our men in a hospitable manner. After remaining all night with them three of the Indians accompanied our hunters to the fort. From these we gathered (through the mulatto who could speak a little of their language) much desired information. The next day myself and the mulatto started to the village, where we arrived about sun half an hour high. We were conducted to the chief's lodge, where we dismounted and were cheerfully saluted by the chief, who was called by the whites "Iron Wristbands" and by the Indians "Pah-dasher-wah-un-dah" or "The Hiding Bear." Our horses were taken to grass and we followed him into his lodge, when he soon ordered supper to be prepared for us. He seemed very much pleased when we told him the whites had built a trading post on Snake River. He said the village would go to the fort in three or four days to trade. We left them next morning loaded with as much fat, dried buffalo meat as our horses could carry, which had been given as a gratuity. We were accompanied on our return to the fort by six of the men. On the 10th the village arrived and pitched their lodges within about 200 yards of the fort. I now commenced learning the Snake language and progressed so far in a short time that I was able to understand most of their words employed in the matters of trade.

October 20th a village of Bannocks consisting of 250 lodges, arrived at the fort. From these we traded a considerable quantity of furs, a large supply of dried meat, deer, elk, and sheep skins. In the meantime we were employed building small log houses and making other necessary preparations for the approaching winter.

CHAPTER III

Snake Valley a Winter Resort for Trappers—Hunting Party Suffers
From Hunger—One Member Lost

November 5th some white hunters arrived at the fort who
had been defeated by the Blackfoot Indians on Ham's Fork of
Green River. One of them had his arm broken by a fusee ball,
but by the salutary relief which he obtained from the fort he
was soon enabled to return to his associates. On the 16th two
more white men arrived and reported that Captain Bonneville
had returned from the lower country and was passing within
thirty miles of the fort on his way to Green River. On the
20th four white men arrived and reported that a party of
the Rocky Mountain Fur Company, consisting of sixty men
under the direction of one of the partners (Mr. Bridger),
were at the forks of Snake River, about sixty miles above the
fort, where they intended to pass the winter. We were also
informed that the two fur companies had formed a coalition.
December 15th the ground was still bare, but frozen, and the
weather very cold. On the 24th Captain Thing arrived from
the mouth of the Columbia with ten men, fetching supplies
for the fort. Times now began to have a different appearance.
The whites and Indians were very numerous in the valley. All
came to pass the winter on the Snake River. On the 20th of

January twelve of Mr. Bridger's men left his camp and came to the fort to get employment. They immediately made an engagement with Captain Thing to form a party for hunting and trapping. On the 15th of March the party was fitted out, consisting of ten trappers and seven camp keepers (myself being one of the latter), under the direction of Mr. Joseph Gale, a native of the City of Washington. March 25th we left the fort and traveled about six miles northeast and encamped on a stream running into the river about twelve miles below the fort, called Portneuf. The next day we followed up this stream in an easterly direction about fifteen miles. Here we found the snow very deep. From this we took a south course in the direction of Bear River. Our animals being so poor and the traveling being so bad, we had to make short marches, and reached Bear River on the 1st day of April. The place where we struck the river was called Cache Valley, so called from its having been formerly a place of deposit for the fur traders. The country on the north and west side of the river was somewhat broken and uneven and covered with wild sage. The snow had disappeared only upon the south sides of the hills. On the south and east sides of the river lay the valley, but it appeared very white and the river nearly overflowing its banks, insomuch that it was very difficult crossing, and should we have been able to have crossed, the snow would have prevented us gaining the foot of the mountain on the east side of the valley. This place being entirely destitute of game, we had to live chiefly upon roots for ten days. On the 11th of April we swam the river with our horses and baggage and pushed our way through the snow across the valley to the foot of the mountain. Here we found the ground bare and dry, but we had to stay another night without supper. About four o'clock the next day the meat of two fat grizzly bears was brought into camp. Our camp kettles had not been greased for some time, as we were continually boiling thistle roots in them during the day, but now four of them containing about three gallons each were soon filled with fat bear meat, cut in very small pieces, and hung over a fire, which all hands were employed in keeping up with the utmost impatience. An old, experienced hand who stood six feet six and was never in a hurry about anything, was selected by a unanimous vote to say when the stew (as we called it) was done, but I thought, with my comrades, that it took a longer time to cook than any meal I ever saw prepared, and after repeated appeals to his long and hungry stewardship by all hands, he at length consented that it might be seasoned with salt and pepper and dished out to cool. But it had not much time for cooling before we commenced operations, and all pronounced it the best meal they had ever eaten, as a matter of course where men had been starving.

The next morning I took a walk up a smooth spur of the mountain to look at the country. This valley commenced about thirty miles below the Soda Springs, the river running west of south entering the valley through a deep cut in the high hills. After winding its way through the north and west borders of the valley, it turned due west and ran through the deep canyon of perpendicular rocks on its way to the

Salt Lake. The valley laid in a sort of semi-circle or rather an oblong on the south and east of about twenty miles in length by five miles in diameter and nearly surrounded by high and rugged mountains from which flowed large numbers of small streams, crossing the valley and emptying into the river. There were large quantities of beaver and otter living in these streams, but the snow melting raised the water so high that our trappers made but slow progress in catching them.

We stopped in this valley until the 20th of April, then moved to the southeast extremity and made an attempt to cross the mountain. The next day we traveled up a stream called Rush Creek in an easterly direction, through a deep gorge in the mountain for about twelve miles, which then widened about a mile into a smooth and rolling country. Here we stayed the following day. We then took a northeast course over the divide and traveled about twelve miles through snow two or three feet deep and in many places drifts to the depth of six or eight feet deep. At night we encamped on a small dry spot of ground on the south side of a steep mountain, where there was little or no vegetation excepting wild sage.

Some time after we had stopped it was disclosed that one man was missing—a young English shoemaker from Bristol. We found he had been seen last dismounted and stopping to drink at a small branch at some distance before we entered the snow. On the following morning I was ordered to go back in search of him. I started on the snow, which was frozen hard enough to bear me and my horse. I went to the place where he was last seen and found his trail, which I followed on to a high mountain, when I lost it among the rocks. I then built a large fire, shot my gun several times, and after hunting till near sunset without hopes of finding him, I gave it up and went to the edge of the snow and stopped for the night. The next morning I started at daylight in a gallop on the snow, traversing mountain and valley smoothed up with snow so hard frozen that a galloping horse scarcely left a foot print. About noon I arrived on a high ridge which over-looked the Snake Lake and the valley southwest of it, which had apparently been clear of snow for some length of time. At the southern extremity of the lake lay the camp, about two miles distant northeast of me. I descended the mountain and entered the camp. On the 27th of April we trave-led down the west side of the lake to the outlet of the Bear River. Here we found about 300 lodges of Snake Indians. We encamped at the village and stayed three days. In the. meantime our trappers were engaged hunting beaver in the river and small streams. We then crossed the river and ascended a branch called Thomas' Fork, in a northerly direction about ten miles. The next day we started across the mountain in a northerly direction and after traveling about five miles we discovered a grizzly bear about 200 yards ahead of us. One of our hunters approached and shot him dead on the spot. We all rode up and dismounted to butcher him. He was an enormous animal, a hideous brute, a savage looking beast. On removing his skin we found the fat on his back measured six inches deep. He had probably not left his winter quarters more than two hours, as we saw his tracks on the snow where he had just left the thick forest of pines on the side of the mountain. We put the meat on our pack animals and traveled up the mountain about five miles and encamped. The next morning we started about two hours before day and crossed the mountain on the snow, which was frozen hard enough to bear our animals, and at ten o'clock AM we found ourselves traveling down a beautiful green vale which led us to the valley of the Salt River, where we encamped about two o'clock PM.

This river derived its name from the numerous salt springs found on its branches. It ran through the middle of a smooth valley about forty miles long and ten wide, emptying its waters into Lewis' Fork of Snake River, its course being almost due north. This was a beautiful valley, covered with green grass and herbage, surrounded by towering mountains covered with snow, spotted with groves of tall spruce pines, which, from their vast elevation, resembled small twigs half immeraed in the snow, whilst thousands of buffaloes carelessly feeding in the green vales contributed to the wild and romantic splendor of the surrounding scenery. On the 10th of May we moved down the river about twelve miles to a stream running into it on the west side called Scott's Fork. Here were some fine salt springs, the salt forming on the pebbles by evaporation to the depth of five or six inches in a short time after the snow had disappeared. May 11th, after gathering a supply of salt, we traveled down the river about fifteen miles and encamped near the mouth of a stream on the west side called

Gardner's Fork. Here we met with Mr. Bridger and his party, who informed us that the country around and below was much infested with Blackfeet. They had several skirmishes with them in which they had lost a number of horses and traps and one young man had been wounded in the shoulder by a ball from a fusee. Upon the receipt of this information our leader concluded to shape his course toward the fort. On the 14th of May we ascended Gardner's Fork about fifteen miles through a deep gorge in the high, craggy mountain. May 15th, traveled up this stream west about ten miles, when the country opened into a valley ten miles long and two wide. Here we left Gardner's Fork, which turns almost due north into the high mountains, with the bend of it just cutting the north end of this valley. We traveled south about three miles and encamped on Blackfoot, which runs into Snake River, after a course of about 100 miles. Here the snow was very deep over nearly the whole plain, which was surrounded by high mountains. On the 16th we traveled down Blackfoot, which runs southwest across the valley, then turns west and runs into a deep cut in the mountain, upwards of a thousand feet above the bed of the stream, the entrance of which seems barely wide enough to admit its waters. We traveled through this canyon for about ten miles, when it opened into a large plain extending to the Sheep Rock on Bear River, which appeared to be about forty miles distant to the southwest. There Blackfoot makes a sweeping curve to the southwest, then gradually turning to the north enters a narrow gorge of basaltic rock, through which it rushes with impetuosity for about fifteen miles, then emerges into the great plain of the Snake River. 17th—We traveled down this stream about fifteen miles and stopped to kill and dry buffalo meat sufficient to load our loose horses. On the 22d we moved down ten miles, where we found thousands of buffalo bulls and killed a great number of them, the cows being very poor at this season of the year. May 30th we traveled down to the plains and on the following day arrived at the fort after traveling about thirty miles in a southwest direction. On arriving at the fort we learned Captain Thing had started in April with twelve men for the purpose of establishing a trading post on a branch of Salmon River, but had been defeated by the Blackfeet, with the total loss of his outfit excepting his men and horses.

CHAPTER IV

Description of a "Fall Hunt"—Abram Patterson Drowned—
Attacked by Indians, One Man Wounded

On the 10th of June a small party belonging to the Hudson Bay Company arrived from Fort Vancouver on the Columbia River, under the direction of Mr. F. Ermatinger, accompanied by Captain William Stewart, an English half--pay officer who had passed the winter at Vancouver and was on a tour of pleasure in the Rocky Mountains. On the 12th they left Fort Hall and started for the grand rendezvous on Green River. We now began to make preparations for what the trappers termed the "Fall Hunt," and all being ready on the 15th, we started. Our party (under our former leader) consisted of twenty-four men, fourteen trappers and ten camp keepers. It was the intention of our leader to proceed to the Yellowstone Lake and hunt the country which lay in the vicinity of our route; from thence proceed to the headwaters of the Missouri and Snake Rivers on our return back to Fort Hall, where it was intended we should arrive about the middle of October next. We traveled up to the mouth of Blackfoot Creek, about ten miles. 16th—Up Blackfoot about fifteen miles. 17th—Followed up this stream about ten miles farther, then left it to our right and took a northeast course through the dry plains covered with dry sage and sand hills, about fifteen miles, to the foot of the mountain and encamped at a small spring which sinks in the plain soon after leaving the mountain. Here we killed a couple of fine bulls and took some of the best meat. 18th—We crossed a low mountain in an easterly direction, about twelve miles, and encamped on a stream called Gray's Creek, which empties into Snake River about forty miles above Fort Hall. 19th—Traveled east over a rough, broken mountainous country about twelve miles and encamped on a branch of the same stream. This country afforded no timber excepting the quaking asp, which grows in small, scrubby groves in the nooks and ravines among the hills. 20th—We left the waters of Gray's Creek and crossed a low place in the mountain in an easterly direction, fell on to a small stream running into Lewis' Fork—distance ten miles. 21st—Traveled east, following this stream to the mouth, about fifteen miles, which was about thirty miles below the mouth of Salt River. Here we were obliged to cross Lewis' Fork, which is about 300 yards wide and might be forded at a low stage of water, but at that time was almost overflowing its banks and running at the rate of about six miles per hour. We commenced making a boat by sewing two raw bull hides together, which we stretched over a frame formed of green willow branches, and then dried it gradually over a slow fire during the night. 22d—Our boat being completed, we commenced crossing our equipage, and while five of us were employed at this a young man by the name of Abram Patterson attempted to cross on horseback. In spite of all the advice and entreaty of those present, his wild and rash temper got the better of his reason and after a desperate struggle to reach the opposite bank he abandoned his horse, made a few springs, and sank to rise no more. He was a native of Pennsylvania, about twenty-three years of age. We succeeded in crossing our baggage and encamped on the east side for the night. Lewis' Fork at this place was timbered with large cottonwood trees along the banks on both sides. On the east lay a valley about twenty-eight miles long and three or four wide in an oblong shape, half enclosed by a range of towering mountains which approached the river at each extremity of the valley. 23d—We crossed the north point of the valley and ascended a small stream about fifteen miles northeast where we encamped among the mountains, thickly covered with tall pines intermingled with fallen timber. 24th—Crossed the mountain, twelve miles easterly course, and descended into the southwest extremity of a valley called Pierre's Hole, where we stayed the next day. This valley lies north and south in an oblong form, about thirty miles long and ten wide, surrounded except on the north by wild and rugged mountains; the east range resembles mountains piled on mountains and capped with three spiral peaks which pierce the clouds. These peaks bear the French name of Tetons or Teats. The Snake Indians called them "The Hoary Headed Fathers." This was a beautiful valley, consisting of a smooth plain intersected by small streams and thickly clothed with grass and herbage and abounding with buffalo, elk, deer, antelope, etc.

On the 27th we traveled to the north end of the valley and encamped on one of the numerous branches which unite at the northern extremity and forms a stream called Pierre's Fork, which discharges its waters into Henry's Fork of Snake River. The stream on which we encamped flows directly from the central Teton and is narrowly skirted with cottonwood trees, closely intermingled with underbrush on both sides. We were encamped on the south side in a place partially clear of brush, under the shade of the large cottonwoods.

On the 28th about nine o'clock AM we were aroused by an alarm of "Indians." We ran to our horses. All was confusion, each trying to catch his horses. We succeeded in driving them into camp, where we caught all but six, which escaped into the prairies. In the meantime the Indians appeared before our camp to the number of sixty, of which fifteen or twenty were mounted on horseback and the remainder on foot, all being entirely naked, armed with fusees, bows, arrows, etc. They immediately caught the horses which had escaped from us and commenced riding to and fro within gunshot of our camp with all the speed their horses were capable of producing, without shooting a single gun, for about twenty minutes, brandishing their war weapons and yelling at the top of their voices. Some had scalps suspended on small poles which they waved in the air, others had pieces of scarlet cloth with one end fastened round their heads while the other trailed after them. After securing my horses I took my gun, examined the priming, set the breech on the ground and hand on the muzzle, with my arms folded, gazed at the novelty of this scene for some minutes, quite unconscious of danger, until the whistling of balls about my ears gave me to understand that these were something more than mere pictures of imagination and gave me assurance that these living creatures were a little more dangerous than those I had been accustomed to see portrayed upon canvas.

The first gun was fired by one of our party, which was taken as the signal for attack on both sides, but the well directed fire from our rifles soon compelled them to retire from the front and take to the brush behind us, where they had the advantage until seven or eight of our men glided into the brush and concealing themselves until their left wing approached within about thirty feet of them before they shot a gun, they then raised and attacked them in the flank. The Indians did not stop to return the fire, but retreated through the brush as fast as possible, dragging their wounded along with them and leaving their dead on the spot. In the meantime myself and the remainder of our party were closely engaged with the center and right. I took advantage of a large tree which stood near the edge of the brush between the Indians and our horses. They approached until the smoke of our guns met. I kept a large German horse pistol loaded by me in case they should make a charge when my gun was empty. When I first stationed myself at the tree I placed a hat on some twigs which grew at the foot of it and would put it in motion by kicking the twigs with my foot in order that they might shoot at the hat and give me a better chance at their heads, but I soon found this was no joke for the poor horses behind me were killed and wounded by the balls intended for me. The Indians stood the fight for about two hours, then retreated through the brush with a dismal lamentation. We then began to look about to find what damage they had done to us. One of our comrades was found under the side of an old root, wounded by balls in three places in the right and one in the left leg below the knee, no bones having been broken. Another had received a slight wound in the groin. We lost three horses killed on the spot and several more were wounded, but not so bad as to be unable to travel. Towards night some of our men followed down the stream about a mile and found the place where they had stopped and laid their wounded comrades on the ground in a circle. The blood was still standing congealed in nine places where they had apparently been dressing the wounds. 29th—Stayed at the same place, fearing no further attempt by the same party of Indians. 30th—Traveled up the main branch about ten miles. July 1st, traveled to the southeast extremity of the valley and encamped for the night. Our wounded comrade suffered very much in riding, although everything was done which lay in our power to ease his sufferings. A pallet was made upon the best gaited horse belonging to the party for him to ride on and one man appointed to lead the animal. On the 2d we crossed the Teton Mountains in an easterly direction, about fifteen miles. The ascent was very steep and rugged, covered with tall pines, but the descent was somewhat smoother.

CHAPTER V

*"Jackson's Hole"—A Dismal Fourth of July Experience Which Is
Terminated Without Serious Mishap—Lost*

Here we again fell on to Lewis's Fork, which runs in a southerly
direction through a valley about eighty miles long, there turning
to the mountains through a narrow cut in the mountain to the
mouth of Salt River, about thirty miles. This valley was called
"Jackson's Hole." It is generally from five to fifteen miles wide.
The southern part where the river enters the mountains is hilly
and uneven, but the northern portion is wide, smooth and comparatively even, the whole being covered with wild sage and surrounded by high and rugged mountains upon whose summit the
snow remains during the hottest months in summer. The alluvial
bottoms along the river and streams intersecting it through the
valley produced a luxuriant growth of vegetation, among which
wild flax and a species of onion were abundant. The great altitude
of this place, however, connected with the cold descending from
the mountains at night, I think would be a serious obstruction to
the growth of most kinds of cultivated grains. This valley, like all
other parts of the country, abounded with game.

Here we again attempted to cross Lewis's Fork with a
bull skin boat. July 4th, our boat being completed. we loaded
it with the baggage and crossed to the other side, but on

returning ran it into some brush, when it instantly filled and sank, but without further accident than the loss of the boat. We had already forded half the distance across the river upon horseback and were now upon an island in the middle, having previously driven our horses to the other shore. We now commenced making a raft of logs that had drifted on the island. On this, when completed, we put the remainder of our equipment about two o'clock PM and ten of us started with it for the other side, but no sooner reached the rapid current than our raft, which was constructed of large timber, became unmanageable and all efforts to reach either side were vain, and, fearing lest we should run on to the dreadful rapids to which we were fast approaching, we abandoned the raft and committed ourselves to the mercy of the current. We being all tolerably good swimmers excepting myself, I would fain have called for help, but at this critical period every one had to shift for himself. Fortunately I scrambled to the shore among the best swimmers. We were now on the side from whence we started without a single article of bedding except an old cloth tent, whilst the rain poured incessantly. Fortunately we had built a large fire previous to our departure on the raft, which was still burning.

I now began to reflect on the miserable condition of myself and those around me—without clothing, provisions or firearms and all drenched to the skin with rain.

I thought of those who were perhaps at that moment celebrating the anniversary of our independence in my native land or seated around tables loaded with the richest dainties that a rich, independent, and enlightened country could afford, or perhaps collected in the gay salon relating the heroic deeds of our ancestors or joining in the nimble dance, forgetful of cares and toils, whilst here presented a group of human beings crouched around a fire which the rain was fast diminishing, meditating on their deplorable condition, not knowing at what moment we might be aroused by the shrill war cry of the hostile savages with which the country was infested, whilst not an article for defense, excepting our butcher knives, remained in our possession.

The night at length came on and we lay down to await the events of the morrow. Daylight appeared and we started down along the shore in hopes of finding something that might get loose from the raft and drift upon the beach. We had not gone a mile when we discovered the raft lodged on a gravel bar which projected from the island, where it had been driven by the current. We hastened through the water waist deep to the spot, where to our great surprise and satisfaction we found everything safe upon the raft in the same manner we had left it. We also discovered that the river, with some difficulty, could be forded on horseback at this place. Accordingly, we had our horses driven across to us, packed them up and mounted, and crossed without further accident, and the day being fair, we spent the remainder of it and the following day drying our equipage. 7th—Left the river and followed up a stream called the Grosbent Fork in an easterly direction about eight miles. This stream was very high and rapid. In fording it we lost two rifles. 8th—We followed the stream through the mountains east, passing through narrow defiles, over rocky precipices and deep gulches for fifteen miles. 9th—Traveled up the stream about ten miles east, then turned up a left hand fork about eight miles northeast and encamped among the high, rough mountains, thickly covered with pine timber. There was not a man in the party who had ever been at this place or at the Yellowstone Lake where we intended to go, but our leader received information from some person at the fort and had written the direction on a piece of paper which he carried with him. They directed us to go from the place where we now were due north, but he said the direction must be wrong, as he could discover no passage through the mountains to the north of us. 10th—We took a narrow defile which led us in an easterly direction about twelve miles, on to a stream running southeast. This we followed down about six miles, when the defile opened into a beautiful valley about fifteen miles in circumference, through which the stream ran in the direction above stated and entered the mountains on the east side. Here a dispute arose about the part of the country we were in. Our leader maintained that this was a branch of the Yellowstone River, but some of the trappers had been in this valley before and knew it to be a branch of Wind River. They pointed out their old encampment and the beaver lodges where they had been trapping two years previous. But our man at the helm was inflexible; he commanded the party and had a right to call these streams by what names he pleased, and as a matter of course this was called the Yellowstone. Three of the party, however, called it

Wind River and left us, but not before one of them had given our charge d'affaires a sound drubbing about some small matters of little importance to anyone but themselves. 11th— We left the stream and crossed the valley in a northeasterly direction, ascended a high point of mountain thickly covered with pines, then descended over cliffs and crags, crossing deep gulches, among the dark forests of pines and logs until about noon, when we came into a smooth, grassy spot about a mile in circumference, watered by a small rivulet which fell from the rocks above, passed through the valley and fell into a chasm on the southeast side among the pines. On the north and west were towering rocks, several thousand feet high, which seemed to overhang this little vale. Thousands of mountain sheep were scattered up and down feeding on the short grass which grew among the cliffs and crevices, some so high that it required a telescope to see them. Our wounded companion suffered severely by this day's travel and our director concluded to remain at this place the next day. He now began to think that these were not the waters of the Yellowstone, as all the branches ran southeast. He finally gave it up and openly declared he could form no distinct idea what part of the country we were in. 12th—Myself and another had orders to mount two of the best mules and ascend the mountain to see if we could find any pass to the northwest of us. We left the camp and traveled in a northerly direction about two miles, then turning to our left around a high point of perpendicular rock entered a narrow glen which led northwest up the mountain. Through this we directed our course, ascending over the loose fragments of rock which had fallen from the dark threatening precipices that seemed suspended in the air above us on either side, for about five miles, when the ascent became so steep that we were obliged to dismount and lead our mules. After climbing about a mile further we came to large banks of snow eight or ten feet deep and so hard that we were compelled to cut steps with our butcher knives to place our feet in, whilst our mules followed in the same track. These places were from fifty to two hundred yards across and so steep that we had to use both hands and feet dog-like in climbing over them. We succeeded in reaching what we at first supposed to be the summit, when another peak appeared in view, completely shrouded with snow, dotted here and there with a few dwarfish, weather-beaten cedars. We now seated ourselves for a few minutes to rest our wearied limbs and gaze on surrounding objects near us. On either hand were large bands of mountain sheep carelessly feeding upon the short grass and herbage which grew among the crags and cliffs, whilst crowds of little lambs were nimbly skipping and playing upon the banks of snow. After resting ourselves a short time, we resumed our march over the snow, leaving the mules behind. We reached the highest summit in about a mile of travel. On the top of this elevation was a flat place of about a quarter of a mile in circumference. On the west and north of us was presented one vast pile of huge mountains crowned with snow, but none appeared so high as the one on which we stood. On the south and east nothing could be seen in the distance but the dense, blue atmosphere.

We did not prolong our stay in this place, for the north wind blew keen and cold as the month of January in a northern climate. We hurried down to where we had left the mules in order to descend to a more temperate climate before the night came on. Our next object was to find a place to descend with our mules, it being impossible to retrace our steps without the greatest danger. After hunting around some time, we at length found a place on the northeast side where we concluded to try it. We drove our mules on to the snow, which being hard and slippery, their feet tripped and after sliding about 300 feet they arrived in a smooth green spot at the foot of the declivity. We then let ourselves down by cutting steps with our butcher knives and the breeches of our guns. After traveling down out of the snow, we encamped on a smooth, green spot and turned our mules loose to feed. At sunset we built a large fire, ate supper and laid down to sleep. The next morning at daybreak I arose and kindled a large fire, and seeing the mules grazing at a short distance, I filled my tobacco pipe and sat down to smoke. Presently I cast my eyes down the mountain and discovered two Indians approaching within 200 yards of us. I immediately aroused my companion, who was still sleeping. We grasped our guns and presented them upon the intruders upon our solitude. They quickly accosted us in the Snake tongue, saying they were Shoshonies and friends to the whites. I invited them to approach and sit down, then gave them some meat and tobacco. They seemed astonished to find us here with mules, saying they knew of but one place where they thought mules or horses could ascend the mountain, and that was in a northeasterly direction. The small stream which was formed by the melting of the snow above us, after running past where we sat rushed down a fearful chasm and was lost in spray. After our visitors had eaten and smoked, we began to question them concerning their families and the country around them. They said their families were some distance below in a northerly direction and that there was a large lake beyond all the snowy peaks in sight to the northwest. They also pointed out the place where we could descend the mountain and told us that this stream ran down through the mountain and united with a larger stream, which, after running a long distance north, turned toward the rising of the sun, into a large plain, where there were plenty of buffalo and Crow Indians. After getting this desired information, we left these sons of the wilderness to hunt their sheep and we went to hunt our camp as we could. We traveled over a high point of rocks composed of granite and coarse sandstone. In many places we saw large quantities of petrifaction, nearly whole trees broken in pieces from one to three feet long completely petrified. We also saw immense pieces of rock on the top of the mountain composed of coarse sand, pebbles and sea shells of various sizes and kinds. After crossing the summit we fell into a defile which led a winding course down the mountain. Near the foot of this defile we found a stone jar which would contain three gallons, neatly cut from a piece of granite, well shaped and smooth. After traveling all day over broken rocks, fallen timber and rough country, we arrived at the camp about dark.

On the 14th we raised camp and traveled north northeast over rough, craggy spurs about fifteen miles and encamped in a narrow glen between two enormous peaks of rocks. As we were passing along over a spur of the mountain we came to a place from which the earth had slid at some previous period and left the steep inclined ledge bare and difficult to cross. Our horses were obliged to place their feet in the small holes and fissures in the rock to keep themselves from sliding off. An unfortunate pack horse, however, missed his footing and slid down the declivity near the brink of a deep and frightful canyon through which the cataract nearby dashed some hundred feet below. Fortunately his foot caught in some roots which projected from a crevice in the rock and arrested his terrible course until we could attach ropes to him and drag him from his perilous situation. 15th—We followed the windings of the glen east as far as we could ride, and then all dismounted and walked except the wounded man, who rode until the mountain became so steep his horse could carry him no longer. We then assisted him from his horse and carried or pushed him to the top of the divide over the snow. In the meantime it commenced snowing very hard. After gaining the summit we unloaded our animals and rushed them on to the snow on the other side, which being hard, they went helterskelter down to a warmer climate and were arrested by a smooth, grassy spot. We then lowered the wounded man down by cords and put our saddles and baggage together on the snow, jumped on the top and started down, slowly at first, but the velocity soon increased until we brought up tumbling heels over head in a grassy bench in a more moderate climate. Now we were down, but whether we could get out was a question yet to be solved. Tremendous, towering mountains of rocks surrounded us excepting on the southeast, where a small stream ran from the snow into a dismal chasm below. But for my part I was well contented, for an eye could scarcely be cast in any direction around, above or below, without seeing the fat sheep gazing at us with anxious curiosity or lazily feeding among the rocks and scrubby pines. The bench where we encamped contained abot 500 acres nearly level. 16th—We stayed at this place, as our wounded comrade had suffered severely the day before. Some went down the stream to hunt a passage, while others went to hunt sheep. Being in camp about ten o'clock I heard the faint report of a rifle overhead. I looked up and saw a sheep tumble down the rocks, which stopped close to where I stood, but the man who shot it had to travel three or four miles before he could descend with safety to the camp. The sheep were all very fat, so that this could be called no other than high living, both as regarded altitude and rich provisions. 17th—Traveled down the stream through difficult and dangerous passage about ten miles, where we struck another branch on the left. This we ascended due north about eight miles and encamped on another green spot near the snow at the head of the glen. 18th—We ascended the mountain at the head of this branch and crossed the divide and descended another branch, which ran in a northerly direction about eight miles, and encamped in an enormous gorge. 19th—Traveled about fifteen miles down stream and encamped on the edge of a plain. 20th—Traveled down to the two forks of this stream, about five miles, and stopped for the night. Here some of the trappers knew the country. This stream was called Stinking River, a branch of the Big Horn, which, after running about forty miles through the big plain, enters the above river about fifteen miles above the lower Big Horn mountain. It takes its name from several hot springs about five miles below the forks, producing a sulphurous stench which is often carried by the wind to the distance of five or six miles. Here were also large quarries of gypsum almost transparent, of the finest quality, and also appearances of lead, with large, rich beds of iron and bituminous coal. We stopped at this place and rested our animals until the 23d. By this time our wounded comrade had recovered so far as to be able to hobble about on crutches.

24th—We took up the right hand fork in a northwesterly direction about fifteen miles, through a rugged defile in the mountain. 25th—Traveled about eighteen miles in the same direction, still following the stream, which ran very rapid down through the dense piles of mountains, which are formed of granite, slate, and stone, covered with pines where there was sufficient soil to support them. 26th—Followed the stream almost due north about eight miles and encamped, where we stayed the next day.

CHAPTER VI

In the Yellowstone Country—A Garden of Eden Inhabited by a
Small Party of Snake Indians

On the 28th we crossed the mountain in a westerly
direction through the thick pines and fallen timber, about
twelve miles, and encamped in a small prairie about a mile
in circumference. Through this valley ran a small stream in
a northerly direction, which all agreed in believing to be a
branch of the Yellowstone. 29th—We descended the stream
about fifteen miles through the dense forest and at length
came to a beautiful valley about eight miles long and three
or four wide, surrounded by dark and lofty mountains. The
stream, after running through the center in a northwesterly
direction, rushed down a tremendous canyon of basaltic rock
apparently just wide enough to admit its waters. The banks of
the stream in the valley were low and skirted in many places
with beautiful cottonwood groves.

Here we found a few Snake Indians comprising six men,
seven women, and eight or ten children, who were the only
inhabitants of the lonely and secluded spot. They were all
neatly clothed in dressed deer and sheep skins of the best quality and seemed to be perfectly contented and happy. They were
rather surprised at our approach and retreated to the heights,

where they might have a view of us without apprehending any danger, but having persuaded them of our pacific intentions we succeded in getting them to encamp with us. Their personal property consisted of one old butcher knife nearly worn to the back, two old, shattered fusees which had long since become useless for want of ammunition, a small stone pot, and about thirty dogs on which they carried their skins, clothing, provisions, etc., on their hunting excursions. They were well armed with bows and arrows pointed with obsidian. The bows were beautifully wrought from sheep, buffalo and elk horns, secured with deer and elk sinews, and ornamented with porcupine quills, and generally about three feet long. We obtained a large number of deer, elk, and sheep skins from them of the finest quality, and three large, neatly dressed panther skins, in return for awls and axes, kettles, tobacco, ammunition, etc. They would throw the skins at our feet and say, "Give us whatever you please for them and we are satisfied; we can get plenty of skins but we do not often see the Tibuboes" (or "People of the Sun"). They said there had been a great many beavers on the branches of this stream, but they had killed nearly all of them, and, being ignorant of the value of fur had singed it off with fire in order to drip the meat more conveniently. They had seen some whites some years previous who had passed through the valley and left a horse behind, but he had died during the first winter. They are never at a loss for fire, which they produce by the friction of two pieces of wood which are rubbed together with a quick and steady motion. One of them drew a map of the country around us on a white elk skin with a piece of charcoal, after which he explained the direction of the different passes, streams, etc. From these we discovered that it was about one day's travel in a south-westerly direction to the outlet or northern extremity of the Yellowstone Lake, but the route, from his description being difficult, and beaver comparatively scarce, our leader gave up the idea of going to it this season, as our horses were much jaded and their feet badly worn. Our geographer also told us that this stream united with the Yellowstone after leaving this valley half a day's travel in a westerly direction. The river then ran a long distance through a tremendous cut in the mountain in the same direction and emerged into a large plain, the extent of which was beyond his geographical knowledge or conception. 30th—We stopped at this place and for my own part I almost wished I could spend the remainder of my days in a place like this, where happiness and contentment seemed to reign in wild, romantic splendor, surrounded by majestic battlements which seemed to support the heavens and shut out all hostile intruders.

Another Man Lost

31st—We left the valley and descended the stream by a narrow, difficult path, winding among the huge fragments of basaltic rock for about twelve miles, when the trail came to an end and the towering rocks seemed to overhang the river on either side, forbidding further progress of man or beast, and obliged us to halt for the night. About dark some of our trappers came to camp and reported one of their comrades to be lost or met with some serious accident. The next day we concluded to stop at this place for the lost man and four men went in search of him, and returned at night without any tidings of him whatever. It was then agreed that either his gun had bursted and killed him or his horse had fallen over some tremendous precipice. He was a man about fifty-five years of age and of thirty years experience as a hunter. Our leader concluded that further search was useless in this rocky, pathless, and pine covered country.

August 2d we forded the Yellowstone with some difficulty to the south side. The river at this place was about 200 yards wide and nearly swimming to the horses. A short distance below it rushes down a chasm with a dreadful roar echoing among the mountains. After crossing we took up a steep and narrow defile in a southerly direction and on gaining the summit in about three miles we found the country to open south and west of us into rolling prairie hills. We descended the mountain and encamped on a small stream running west. 3d—Traveled about twenty-five miles due west, the route broken and uneven in the latter part of the day, and in some places thickly covered with pines. Encamped at night in a valley called "Gardner's Hole." This valley was about forty miles in circumference, surrounded, except on the north and west, by low, puny mountains. On the west was a high, narrow range of mountains running north and south, dividing the waters of the Yellowstone from those of the Gallatin Fork of the Missouri. We stopped in this valley until the 20th, the trappers being continually employed in hunting and trapping beaver.

On the 21st we crossed the mountains through a defile in a westerly direction and fell on to a small branch of the Gallatin. Here we encamped on a small clear spot and killed the fattest elk I ever saw. It was a large bull. The fat on his rump measured seven inches thick. He had fourteen spikes on the left horn and twelve on the right. 22d—After we had started in the morning, five of our party (four trappers and one camp tender) secretly dropped behind with their packs and riding horses and took a different direction, forming a party of their own, but they could not be much blamed for leaving, as our fractious leader was continually wrangling with the trappers by endeavoring to excrcise his authority tyranically. We followed down this branch to the Gallatin, about ten miles west, encamped and stayed the next day. 24th—Down the Gallatin north northwest, the river running between two high ranges of mountains, skirted along the bank by a narrow valley. 25th—Left the defile and took up the Gallatin in an easterly direction, crossed the mountain and fell on to a stream running into the Yellowstone, and finding no beaver, returned to the Gallatin the next day the route we had come. 28th—Up the Gallatin to the place where we had struck it on the 22d. 29th—Took up the stream a southerly course about ten miles, then left it to the left hand and proceeded about four miles south through a low pass and fell on to a branch of the Madison Fork of the Missouri running south. This we followed down about six miles further and encamped, where we stayed next day. This pass was formed by the minor ranges of hills or spurs on the two high ranges of mountains on either side of us, which approach toward each other and terminate in a low defile completely covered with pines except along the stream, where small prairies may be found thickly clothed with grass, forming beautiful encampments.

CHAPTER VII

Encounter With Blackfeet Indians—Join Bridger's Party for
Protection and Assistance

31st—Traveled southwest down the stream about ten miles, when we came to the "Burnt Hole," a prairie valley about eighty miles in circumference, surrounded by low spurs of pine-covered mountains which are the sources of great numbers of streams which by uniting in this valley form the Madison Fork. Sept. 1st—Traveled down the stream about twelve miles northwest and encamped during a heavy snow-storm. This stream, after leaving the valley, enters a gorge in the mountains in a northwesterly direction. 2d—We stopped in the entrance of this gorge until the 8th. Traveled down about fifteen miles, where the country opened into a large plain, through which the stream turned in a sweeping curve due north. 9th—Crossed the valley in a westerly direction, traveled up a small branch and encamped about three miles from the river in a place with high bluffs on each side of us. We had been encamped about an hour when fourteen white trappers came to us in full gallop. They were of Mr. Bridger's party, who was encamped at Henry's Lake, about twenty miles in a southerly direction, and expected to arrive at the Madison the next day. His party consisted of sixty white men and about twenty Flathead Indians. These trappers remained with us during the night, telling mountain "yarns" and the news from the States. Early next morning eight of them started down the stream to set traps on the main fork, but returned in about an hour closely pursued by about eighty Blackfeet. We immediately secured our horses in a yard previously made for the purpose, and prepared for battle. In the meantime the Indians had gained the bluffs and commenced shooting into the camp from both sides. The bluff on the east side was very steep and rocky, covered with tail pines, the foot approaching within forty yards of us. On the west the bluffs were covered with thick groves of quaking asps. From these heights they poured in fusee balls without mercy or even damage, except killing our animals which were exposed to their fire. In the meantime we concealed ourselves in the thicket around the camp to await a nearer approach, but they were too much afraid of our rifles to come near enough for us to use ammunition. We lay almost silently about three hours, when finding they could not arouse us to action by their long shots, they commenced setting fire to the dry grass and rubbish with which we were surrounded. The wind blowing brisk from the south, in a few moments the fire was converted into one circle of flame and smoke which united over our heads. This was the most horrible position I was ever placed in. Death seemed almost inevitable, but we did not despair, and all hands began immediately to remove the rubbish around the encampment and setting fire to it to act against the flames that were hovering over our heads. This plan proved successful beyond our expectations. Scarce half an hour had elapsed when the fire had passed around us and driven our enemies from their position. At length we saw an Indian whom we supposed to be the chief standing on a high point of rock and giving the signal for retiring, which was done by taking hold of the opposite corners of his robe, lifting it up and striking it three times on the ground. The cracking of guns then ceased and the party moved off in silence. They had killed two horses and one of the mules on the spot and five more were badly wounded. It was about four o'clock in the afternoon when the firing ceased. We then saddled and packed our remaining animals and started for Mr. Bridger's camp, which we found on the Madison at the place where we had left it. Our party was now so disabled from the previous desertion of men and loss of animals that our leader concluded to travel with Mr. Bridger until we should arrive at the forks of the Snake River, where the latter intended to pass the winter.

On the 11th myself with five others returned to the battle ground to get some traps which had been set for beaver on the stream above our encampment, whilst the main camp was to travel down the river about five miles and stop the remainder of the day to await our return. We went for the traps and returned to the camp about three o'clock PM. 12th—At sunrise an alarm of "Blackfeet!" echoed through the camp. In a moment all were under arms and inquiring "Where are they?" when 'twas replied, "On the hills to the west." I cast a glance along the high range of hills which projected toward the river from the mountain and discovered them standing in a line on a ridge. In their center stood a small pole and from it waved an American flag, displaying a wish to make peace. About thirty of us walked up within about 300 yards of their line, when they made a signal for us to halt and send two men to meet the same number of theirs and treat for peace. Two of the whites who could speak the Blackfoot language were appointed to negotiate, while the respective lines sat upon the ground to await the event. After talking and smoking for half an hour the negotiators separated and returned to their respective parties. Ours reported them to be a party of Pagans, a small tribe of the Blackfeet, who desired to make peace with the whites and for that purpose had procured the flag from an American trading post on the Missouri. There were forty-five members, well armed and equipped. We gave them a general invitation to our camp, which they accepted with a great deal of reluctance, when they were informed of the battle on the 10th, but arriving at the camp and receiving friendly treatment, their fears in a manner subsided. After smoking several rounds of the big pipe, the chief began to relate his adventures. He said he had been in several battles with the whites and some of the party were at the battle in "Pierre's Hole" on the 28th of June, last, in which there were four Indians killed on the spot and eight died of their wounds on the way to the village, but he denied having any knowledge of the late battle, but said there were several parties of the Blood Indians lurking about the mountains around us. They stopped with us until nearly night and all left except one, who concluded to remain. 13th—We left the Madison

Fork with Mr. Bridger's camp and ascended a small branch in a westerly direction through the mountains about twenty miles, and encamped on the divide. After we had encamped a Frenchman started down the mountain to set his traps for beaver, contrary to the advice and persuasion of his comrades. He had gone but a few miles when he was fired upon by a party of Blackfeet, killed and scalped.

On the 14th we traveled down the mountain about fifteen miles northwest, and encamped on a stream called "Stinking Creek," which runs into the Jefferson Fork of the Missouri. After we had encamped some trappers ascended the stream, but were driven back by the Blackfeet. Others went below and shared the same fate from another party, but escaped to the camp unhurt. 15th—Moved down this stream about twelve miles north. This part of the country was comprised of high, bald hills on either side of the stream, which terminated in rough, pine-covered mountains. 16th—We traveled down the stream northwest about eight miles. The valley opened wider as we descended, and large numbers of buffalo were scattered over the plains and among the hills. 17th—Down about ten miles northwest, the mountains on the west side descending to a sloping spur, from thence to a plain. 18th—We did not raise camp, and about noon some Flathead Indians arrived and told us their village was on a branch of the Jefferson called "Beaverhead Creek," about thirty miles in a westerly direction. The next day we went to their village, which consisted of 180 lodges of Flatheads and Pend d'Oreilles (or Hanging Ears). Here we found a trading party belonging to the Hudson Bay Conpamy. They were under the direction of Mr. Francis Ermatinger, who was endeavoring to trade every beaver skin as fast as they were taken from the water by the Indians. 20th—The whole cavalcade moved en masse up the stream about twelve miles southwest and encamped with another village of the same tribe consisting of 130 lodges.

From this place was a large plain, slightly undulating, extending nearly to the junction of the three forks of the Missouri. The Flatheads were a brave, friendly, generous and hospitable tribe, strictly honest, with a mixture of pride which exalts them far above the rude appelation of savages, when contrasted with the tribes around them. They boast of never injuring the whites and consider it a disgrace to their tribe if they are not treated like brothers whilst in company with them. Sorcery, fornication, and adultery are severely punished. Their chiefs are obeyed with a reverence due to their station and rank.

23d—We left the village in company with Mr. Bridger and his party and traveled southeast across the plain about six miles to the foot of the hills and encamped at a spring. 24th—Traveled about eighteen miles southeast over high, rolling hills, beautifully clothed with bunch grass. 25th—Traveled in the same direction twelve miles and encamped in a smooth valley about eighty miles in circumference, surrounded on the north and east by a high range of mountains. At the northeast extremity was a marshy lake about twelve miles in circumference. From this flowed the head stream of the Jefferson Fork of the Missouri, which curved to the southwest through the valley and entered the low mountains on the west through a narrow cut, still continuing the curve encircling a large portion of country previous to its arrival at the junction. 26th—Crossed the valley about sixteen miles and encamped on the east side. This valley, as a mountaineer would say, was full of buffalo when we entered it and large numbers of them were killed by our hunters. We repeatedly saw signs of Blackfeet about us to waylay the trappers. 27th— We stopped at this place and encamped on Camas Creek on the northwest extremity of the great plain of the Snake River. Here the leader of our party desired me to go to Fort Hall and get some horses to assist them to the fort, as we were dependent on Mr. Bridger for animals to move camp.

CHAPTER VIII

Dispatched for Horses—Perfidy of Leader Suspected—Two Days
Without Water—Finally Reaches For Hall

30th—After getting the necessary information from our leader, I started, contrary to the advice and remonstrances of Mr. Bridger and his men, rather than be impeached of cowardice by our autocratic director. I traveled according to his directions south until dark amid thousands of buffaloes. The route was very rocky and my horse's feet (he not being shod) were worn nearly to the quick, which caused him to limp very much. After traveling about thirty miles I lay down and slept sound during the night. The next morning I arose and proceeded on my journey down the stream. About nine o'clock I came to where it formed a lake, where it sank in the dry and sandy plain. From this I took a southeasterly course, as directed, towards a high butte which stood in the almost barren plain. By passing to the east of this butte, I was informed that it was about twenty-five miles to Snake River. In this direction I traveled until about two hours after dark. My horse had been previously wounded by a ball in the loins, and though nearly recovered before I started, yet traveling over the rocks and gravel with tender feet and his wound together had nearly exhausted him. I turned him loose among the rocks and wild sage and laid myself down to meditate on the follies of myself and others. In about two hours I fell asleep to dream of cool springs, rich feasts and cool shade. In the morning I arose and looked around me. My horse was near by me picking the scanty blades of sunburned grass which grew among the sage. On surveying the place I found I could go no further in a south or east direction, as there lay before me a range of broken, basaltic rock which appeared to extend for five or six miles on either hand and five or six miles wide, thrown together promiscuously in such a manner that it was impossible for a horse to cross them. The butte stood to the southwest about ten miles, which I was informed was about half the distance from Camas Lake to Snake River. I now found that either from ignorance or some other motive less pure, our leader had given me directions entirely false, and came to the conclusion to put no further confidence in what he had told me, but return to the lake I had left, as it was the nearest water I knew of. This point being settled, I saddled my horse and started on foot, leading him by the bridle, and traveled all day in the direction of the lake over the hot sand and gravel. After daylight disappeared I took a star for my guide, but it led me south of the lake, where I came on to several large bands of buffalo, which would start on my near approach and run in all directions. It was near midnight when I laid down to rest. I had plenty of provisions, but could not eat. Water! Water was the object of my wishes. Traveling for two days in the hot burning sun without water is by no means a pleasant way of passing the time. I soon fell asleep and dreamed again of bathing in the cool rivulets issuing from the snow topped mountains. About an hour before day I was awakened by the howling of wolves, they having formed a complete circle within thirty paces of me and my horse. At the flashing of my pistol, however, they soon dispersed. At daylight I discovered some willows about three miles distant to the west, where large numbers of buffalo had assembled, apparently for water. In two hours I had dispersed the brutes and lay by the water side. After drinking and bathing for half an hour, I traveled up the stream about a mile and lay down among some willows to sleep in the shade, whilst my horse was carelessly grazing among the bushes. The next day being the 4th, I lay all day and watched the buffalo, which were feeding in immense bands all about me.

5th—I arose in the morning, at sunrise and looking to the southwest I discovered the dust arising in a defile which led through the mountain about five miles distant. The buffaloes were carelessly feeding all over the plain as far as the eye could reach. I watched the motion of the dust for a few minutes, when I saw a body of men on horseback pouring out of the defile among the buffalo. In a few minutes the dust rose to the heavens. The whole mass of buffalo became agitated, producing a sound resembling distant thunder. At length an Indian pursued a cow close to me. Running alongside of her he let slip an arrow and she fell. I immediately recognized him to be a Bannock with whom I was acquainted. On discovering me he came to me and saluted me in Snake, which I answered in the same tongue. He told me the village would come and encamp where I was. In the meantime he pulled off some of his clothing and hung it on a stick as a signal for the place where his squaw should set his lodge. He then said he had killed three fat cows but would kill one more and stop. So saying he wheeled his foaming charger and the next moment disappeared in the cloud of dust. In about half an hour the old chief came up with the village and invited me to stop with him, which I accepted. While the squaws were putting up and stretching their lodges, I walked out with the chief on to a small hillock to view the field of slaughter, the cloud of dust having passed away, and the prairie was covered with the slain. Upward of one thousand cows were killed without burning one single grain of gunpowder. The village consisted of 332 lodges and averaged six persons, young and old, to each lodge. They were just returning from the salmon fishing to feast on fat buffalo. After the lodges were pitched I returned to the village. This chief was called "Aikenlo-ruckkup" (or "The Tongue Cut With a Flint"). He was the brother of the celebrated Horn Chief, who was killed in a battle with the Blackfeet some years before, and it was related by the Bannocks, without the least scruple, that he was killed by a piece of antelope horn, the only manner in which he could have been taken, as he was protected by a supernatural power from all other harm. My worthy host spared no pains to make my situation as comfortable as his circumstances would permit. The next morning I took a walk through the village and found there were fifteen lodges of Snakes with whom I had formed an acquaintance the year before. On my first entering the village I was informed that two white trappers belonging to Mr. Wyeth's party had been lately killed by the Bannocks in the lower country and that the two Indians who had killed or caused them to be killed were then in the village. The old chief had pointed them out to me as we walked through the village and asked me what the white men would do about it. I told him they would hang them if they caught them at the fort. He said it was good; that they deserved death, for said he, "I believe they have murdered the two white men to get their property, and lost it all in gambling, for," continued he, "ill gained wealth often flies away and does the owners no good. But," said he, "you need not be under any apprehension of danger whilst you stop with the village." The squaws were employed cutting and drying meat for two days. at the end of which time the ground on which the village stood seemed covered with meat scaffolds bending beneath their rich loads of fat buffalo meat.

13th—My horse being somewhat recruited, I left the village with a good supply of boiled buffalo tongue prepared by my landlady, and the necessary directions and precautions from the old chief. I traveled due east about twenty-five miles, which brought me to the forks of Snake River. When approaching to the waters I discovered fresh human footprints. I immediately turned my horse and rode out from the river about a quarter of a mile, intending to travel parallel with the river in order to avoid any straggling party of Blackfeet, which might be secreted in the timber growing along the bank. I had not gone far when I discovered three Indians on horseback running a bull toward me. I jumped my horse into a ravine and out of sight and crawled up among the high sage to watch their movements. As they approached nearer to me I saw they were Snakes and showed myself to them. They left the bull and galloped up to me. After the usual salutation, I followed them to their village, which was on the east bank of the river. The village consisted of fifteen lodges under the direction of a chief called "Comb Daughter" by the Snakes and by the whites "Lame Chief." He welcomed me to his lodge in the utmost good humor and jocular manner I had ever experienced among the Indians, and I was sufficiently acquainted with the Snake language to repay his jokes in his own coin without hesitation. I passed the time very agreeably for six days among these simple but well-fed and good-humored savages.

On the 19th, learning that Bridger was approaching the forks and the party of hunters to which I had belonged had passed down the river toward the fort, I mounted my horse, started down the river and arrived at the fort next day about noon, the distance being about sixty miles south southwest.

When I arrived the party had given up all hopes of ever seeing me again and had already fancied my lifeless body lying on the plains, after having been scalped by the savages.

CHAPTER IX

The time for which myself and all of Mr. Wyeth's
men were engaged had recently expired, so that now I was
independent of the world and no longer to be termed a
"greenhorn." At least I determined not to be so green as to
bind myself to an arbitrary Rocky Mountain Chieftain to be
kicked over hill and dale at his pleasure.

November 15th Captain Thing arrived from the Columbia
with supplies for the fort. In the meantime the men about the
fort were doing nothing and I was lending them a hand until
Mr. Wyeth should arrive and give us our discharge.

December 20th Mr. Wyeth arrived, when I bid adieu to
the "Columbia River Fishing and Trading Company" and
started, in company with fifteen of my old messmates, to
pass the winter at a place called "Mutton Hill," on Portneuf,
about forty miles southeast from Fort Hall. Mr. Wyeth had
brought a new recruit of sailors and Sandwich islanders to
supply our places at the fort. We lived on fat mutton until the
snow drove us from the mountains in February. Our party
then dispersing, I joined Mr. Bridger's company, who were
passing the winter on Blackfoot Creek, about fifteen miles
from the fort, where we stayed until the latter part of March.

Mr. Bridger's men lived very poor and it was their own fault, for the valley was covered with fat cows when they arrived in November, but instead of approaching and killing their meat for the winter they began to kill by running on horseback, which had driven the buffalo all over the mountain to the head of the Missouri, and the snow falling deep, they could not return during the winter. They killed plenty of bulls, but they were so poor that their meat was perfectly blue, yet this was their only article of food, as bread and vegetables were out of the question in the Rocky Mountains, except a few kinds of roots of spontaneous growth, which the Indians dig and prepare for food. It would doubtless be amusing to a disinterested spectator to witness the process of cooking poor bull meat as practiced by this camp during the winter of 1835–6. On going through the camp at any time in the day heaps of ashes might be seen with the fire burning on the summit and an independent looking individual, who is termed a camp kicker, sitting with a "two-year-old club" in his hand watching the pile with as much seeming impatience as Philoctele did the burning of Hercules. At length, poking over the ashes with his club, it bounds five or six feet from the ground like a huge ball of gum elastic. This operation, frequently repeated, divests the ashes adhering to it and prepares it for carving. He then drops his club and draws his butcher knife calling to his comrades, "Come Major, Judge, Squire, Dollar, Pike, Cotton, and Gabe, won't you take a lunch of Simon?" each of whom acts according to the dictates of his appetite in accepting or refusing the invitation. I have often witnessed these philosophical and independent dignitaries collected round a bull's ham just torn from a pile of embers, good-humoredly observing as they hacked the huge slices from the lean mass that this was tough eating but that it was tougher where there was none, and consoling themselves with a promise to make the fat cows suffer before the year rolled around. The camp remained on Blackfoot until the latter part of March, when the winter broke up and we commenced traveling and hunting beaver.

We left winter quarters on the 28th and traveled along the foot of the mountain in a northerly direction to Lewis Fork and ascended it southeast to the mouth of Muddy Creek, where we arrived on the 7th of April. Here Mr. Bridger ordered a party of twelve trappers to branch off to the right and hunt the head waters of Gray and Blackfoot Creeks. I was included in the number and felt anxious to try my skill in trapping.

10th—We set off, leaving the main camp, to proceed leisurely to Saltrim valley and from thence to the mouth of Thomas Fork of Bear River, where we were instructed to meet them. We ascended Muddy Creek and crossed the mountain on to Gray's Creek. Here we found the snow disappearing very fast and the streams so much swollen that we made but slow progress in taking beaver. We traveled the numerous branches of this stream to and fro, setting traps where the water would permit, until the 25th of April, when we left the waters of Gray's Creek and traveled about forty miles in a southwest direction from where we had struck it, crossed a low mountain about eight miles and fell on to Blackfoot. This we ascended two days and hunted until the 5th of May, when three of our party were waylaid and fired upon by a party of Blackfeet whilst ascending the stream through a canyon. One of them was slightly wounded in the side by a fusee ball, but all escaped to the camp and reported the Indians to be about twenty-five in number. On the 7th of May we left Blackfoot and crossed the mountain southwest through deep snow and thick pines and at night fell into the valley on Bear River and encamped about twenty-five miles above the soda springs. 8th—Traveled up Bear River to Thomas Fork, where we found the main camp, likewise Mr. A. Dripps and his party, consisting of about sixty whites and nearly as many half breeds, who were encamped with 400 lodges of Snakes and Bannocks and 100 lodges of Nez Perces and Flatheads. 9th—We all camped together in the beautiful plain on Bear River above the mouth of Smiths Fork. 11th-The whole company of Indians and whites left Bear River and traveled to Ham's Fork, excepting Mr. Dripps and a small party, who went round to Black's Fork of Green River to get some furs and other articles deposited there in the ground. After reaching Ham's Fork the Indians concluded to separate in diffferent directions, as we were in too large a body and had too many horses to thrive long together. They were instructed to be on the mouth of Horse Creek on Green River about the 1st of July, as we expected supplies from the United States about that time. We laid about on the branches of Green River until the 28th of June. when we arrived at the destined place of rendezvous. On the 1st of July Mr. Wyeth arrived from the mouth of the Columbia on his way to the United States, with a small party of men.

CHAPTER X

Rendezvous at Green River—Meeting Revs. Whitman and Spaulding and Their Wives on Their Way to Oregon

On the 3rd the outfit arrived from St. Louis, consisting of forty men having twenty horse carts drawn by mules and loaded with the supplies for the ensuing year. They were accompanied by Doctor Marcus Whitman and lady, Mr. H.H. Spaulding and lady, and Mr. W.H. Gray, Presbyterian missionaries, on their way to the Columbia to establish a mission among the Indians in that quarter. The two ladies were gazed on with wonder and astonishment by the rude savages, they being the first white women ever seen by these Indians and the first that had ever penetrated into these wild and rocky regions.

We remained at the rendezvous until the 16th of July and then began to branch off into parties for the fall hunt in different directions.

Mr. Bridger's party, as usual, was destined for the Blackfoot country. It contained most of the American trappers and amounted to sixty men. I started with a party of fifteen trappers and two camp keepers, ordered by Mr. Bridger to proceed to the Yellowstone Lake and there await his arrival with the rest of the party. July 24th we set off and traveled up Green River twenty-five miles in a northerly direction.

25th—Up Green River fifteen miles in the same direction, then left it to our right and took up a small branch, keeping a northeast course still. The course of the river where we left it turns abruptly to the east and heads in a high, craggy mountain, covered with snow, about thirty miles distant. This mountain is a spur of the Wind River range and is commonly called the Sweetwater mountain, as that stream heads in its southern termination. After leaving the river we traveled about four miles to the head of the branch and encamped in a smooth, grassy plain on the divide between Green and Snake Rivers, which head within 200 paces of each other at this place. 26th—Traveled north about fifteen miles, descending a small stream through a rough, mountainous country covered with pine trees and underbrush, and encamped on Grosvent Fork. 27th—We descended the Grosvent Fork to "Jackson's Hole" about twenty miles, general course west. 28th—We followed Lewis Fork through the valley, crossing several large streams coming in from the east. We then left the valley and followed the river about five miles through a piece of rough, piney country, and came to Jackson's Lake, which is formed by the river. We encamped at the outlet at a small prairie about a mile in circumference. This lake is about twenty-five miles long and three miles wide, lying north and south, bordered on the east by pine swamps and marshes extending from one to two miles from the lake, to the spurs of the mountain. On the southwest stands the three Tetons, whose dark, frightful forms rising abruptly from the lake, towering above the clouds, cast a gloomy shade upon the waters beneath, whilst the water rushes in torrents down the awful precipices from the snow by which they are crowned. The high range of mountains on the west, after leaving the Tetons, slope gradually to the north and spread into low piney mountains. This place, like all other marshes and swamps among the mountains, is infested with innumerable swarms of horseflies and mosquitoes, to the great annoyance of man and beast during the day, but the cold air descending from the mountain at night compels them to seek shelter among the leaves and grasses at an early hour. Game is plentiful and the river and lake abound with fish. After hunting the streams and marshes about this lake, we left it on the 7th of August and traveled down Lewis Fork about four miles to the second stream running into it on the east side below the lake. This we ascended about twelve miles east and encamped among the pines close to where it emerged from a deep canyon in the mountain. 8th—We took across a high spur thickly covered with pines, intermingled with brush and fallen timber, in a northeast direction for about twelve miles, where we fell into a small valley on a left hand branch of the stream we had left. 9th—We took up this branch due north about ten miles, when, it turning short to the right, we left it and ascended a narrow glen, keeping a north course, sometimes traveling through thick pines and then crossing small green spots through which little streams were running from the remaining banks of snow lying among the pines in the shade of the mountains, for about six miles, when we came to a smooth prairie about two miles long and half a mile wide, lying east and west, surrounded by pines. On the south side, about midway of the prairie, stood a high snowy peak from whence issued a stream of water which, after entering the plain, divided equally, one-half running west and the other east, thus bidding adieu to each other, one bound for the Pacific and the other for the Atlantic ocean. Here a trout of twelve inches in length may cross the mountains in safety. Poets have sung of the "meeting of the waters" and fish climbing cataracts, but the "parting of the waters and fish crossing mountains," I believe, remains unsung as yet by all except the solitary trapper who sits under the shade of a spreading pine whistling blank verse and beating time to the tune with a whip on his trap sack whilst musing on the parting advice of those waters. 10th—We took down the east branch and followed it about eight miles to the Yellowatone River, which is about eighty yards wide and at the shallowest place nearly swimming to our horses. To this place it comes from a deep gorge in the mountains, enters a valley lying north and south about fifteen miles long and three miles wide, through which it winds its way slowly to the north through swamps and marshes and calmly reposes in the bosom of the Yellowstone Lake. The south extremity of this valley was smoother and thickly clothed with high meadow grass, surrounded by high, craggy mountains, topped with snow. We stopped at this place trapping until the 3d of August, when we traveled down the lake to the inlet or southern extremity.

CHAPTER XI

Interesting Description of What is Known as Yellowstone National Park

16th—Mr. Bridger came up with the remainder of the party. 18th—The whole camp moved down the east shore of the lake through thick pines and fallen timber about eighteen miles and encamped in a small prairie. 19th—Continued down the shore to the outlet about twenty miles, and encamped in a beautiful plain which extended along the northern extremity of the lake. This valley was interspersed with scattering groves of tall pines, forming shady retreats for the numerous elk and deer during the heat of the day. The lake is about 100 miles in circumference, bordered on the east by high ranges of mountains whose spurs terminate at the shore and on the west by a low bed of piney mountains. Its greatest width is about fifteen miles, lying in an oblong form south to north, or rather in the shape of a crescent. Near where we encamped were several hot springs which boiled perpetually. Near these was an opening in the ground about eight inches in diameter from which hot steam issued continually with a noise similar to that made by the steam issuing from the safety valve of an engine, and could be heard five or six miles distant. I should think the steam issued with sufficient force to work an engine of thirty horsepower. We encamped about three o'clock PM and after resting our horses about an hour, seven of us were ordered to go out and hunt some streams running into the Yellowstone some distance below the lake. We started from the camp in an easterly direction, crossed the plain and entered the pines, and after traveling about an hour through dense forests we fell into a broken tract of country which seemed to be all on fire at some distance below the surface. It being very difficult to get around this place, we concluded to follow an elk trail across it for about half a mile. The treading of our horses sounded like traveling on a plank platform covering an immense cavity in the earth, whilst the hot water and steam were spouting and hissing around us in all directions. As we were walking and leading our horses across this place, the horse that was before me broke through the crust with one hind foot and the blue steam rushed forth from the hole. The whole place was covered with a crust of lime stone of a dazzling whiteness, formed by the overflowing of the boiling water. Shortly after leaving this resemblance of the infernal regions, we killed a fat elk and camped at sunset in a smooth, grassy spot between two high, shaggy ridges, watered by a small stream which came tumbling down the gorge behind us. As we had passed the infernal regions we thought, as a matter of course, this must be a commencement of the Elysian Fields, and accordingly commenced preparing a feast. A large fire was soon blazing, encircled with sides of elk ribs and meat cut in slices, supported on sticks, down which the grease ran in torrents. The repast being over, the jovial tale goes round the circle, the peals of loud laughter break upon the stillness of the night which, after being mimicked in the echo from rock to rock dies away in the solitary gloom. Every tale reminds an auditor of something similar to it but under different circumstances, which, being told, the "laughing part" gives rise to increasing merriment and furnishes more subjects for good jokes and witty sayings such as a Swift never dreamed of. Thus the evening passed, with eating, drinking, and stories, enlivened with witty humor until near midnight, all being wrapped in their blankets lying round the fire, gradually falling to sleep one by one, until the last tale is encored by the snoring of the drowsy audience. The speaker takes the hint, breaks off the subject and wrapping his blanket more closely about him, soon joins the snoring party. The light of the fire being superseded by that of the moon just rising from behind the eastern mountain, a sullen gloom is cast over the remaining fragments of the feast and all is silent except the occasional howling of the solitary wolf on the neighboring mountain, whose senses are attracted by the flavor of roasted meat, but fearing to approach nearer, he sits upon a rock and bewails his calamities in piteous moans which are reechoed among the mountains.

Aug. 20th—Took over a high, rugged mountain about twelve miles northeast and fell into the secluded valley which I have described in my last year's journal. There we found some of those indifferent and happy natives of whom I gave a description. We traded some beaver and dressed skins from them and hunted the streams running into the valley for several days. There is something in the wild, romantic scenery of this valley which I cannot, nor will I attempt, to describe, but the impressions made upon my mind while gazing from a high eminence on the surrounding landscape one evening as the sun was gently gliding behind the western mountains and casting its gigantic shadow across the vale were such as time can never efface from my memory, but as I am neither poet, painter nor romance writer I must content myself to be what I am—a humble journalist—and leave this beautiful vale in obscurity until visited by some more skillful admirer of the beauties of nature who may chance to stroll this way at some future period.

25th—Left the valley and traveled down to the Yellowstone and crossed it at the ford. 26th—Crossed the mountain in a southwest direction and fell on to Gardner's Fork. Here myself and another set some traps and stopped for the night whilst the remainder of the party went in different directions to hunt setting. 27th—We crossed the mountain southwest to "Gardner's Hole," where we found the main camp. 28th—Camp left "Gardner's Hole" and traveled north to the Yellowstone about twenty miles. 29th—The whole party followed the river out of the mountain into the great Yellowstone plain, distance about twelve miles. The trappers then scattered out in small parties of from two to five in number, leaving Mr. Bridger with twenty-five camp keepers to travel slowly down the river. Myself and another traveled down the river about forty miles northeast to a branch called "Twenty-five Yard River," This we ascended about twenty-five miles in a northerly direction, where we remained trapping several days. The country lying on this stream is mostly comprised of high rolling ridges, thickly clothed with grass and herbage and crowded with immense bands of buffalo, intermingled with bands of antelope.

CHAPTER XII

Laughable and Serious Engagements With Bands of Blackfeet Indians—"Howell's Encampment."

Sept. 1st—We returned to the camp, which we found at the mouth of this stream, where we found also ten Delaware Indians who had joined the camp in order to hunt beaver with greater security. 2d—Traveled down the Yellowstone River about twenty miles. This is a beautiful country, the large plains widely extending on either side of the river, intersected with streams and occasional low spurs of mountains, whilst thousands of buffaloes may be seen in almost every direction, and deer, elk, and grizzly bear are abundant. The latter are more numerous than in any other part of the mountains, owing to the vast quantities of cherries, plums, and other wild fruits which this section of the country affords. In going to visit my traps, a distance of three or four miles, early in the morning, I have frequently seen seven or eight standing about the clumps of cherry bushes on their hind legs, gathering cherries with surprising dexterity, not even deigning to turn their grizzly heads to gape at the passing trapper, but merely casting a sidelong glance at him without altering their position. 3d—Left the camp on the Yellowstone and started across a low and somewhat broken tract of country in a southeasterly direction to a stream called the Rosebud, accompanied by another trapper. 5th—The camp came to us on the Rosebud and the next day passed on in the same direction, whilst myself and comrade stopped behind to trap. 7th—We overtook the camp on a stream called Rocky Fork, a branch of Clark's Fork of the Yellowstone. When we arrived at camp we were told the sad news of the death of a French trapper named Bodah, who had been waylaid and killed by a party of Blackfeet while setting his traps, and one of the Delawares had been shot through the hip by the rifle of one of his comrades going off accidentally, and several war parties of Blackfeet had been seen scouting about the country. We had been in camp but a few minutes when two trappers rode up whom we called "Major Meek" and "Dave Crow." The former, a tall Virginian who had been in the mountains some twelve years, was riding a white Indian pony. On dismounting some blood was discovered which had apparently been running down his horse's neck and dried on the hair. He was immediately asked where he had been and what was the news. "News!" exclaimed he, "I have been, me and Dave, over on to Prior's Fork to set our traps and found old Benj. Johnson's boys over there, just walking up and down them 'ar streams with their hands on their hips gathering plums. They gave me a tilt, and turned me a somerset or two, shot my horse, 'Too Shebit,' in the neck and sent us heels over head in a pile together, but we raised a-runnin'. Gabe, do you know where Prior leaves the cut bluffs, goin' up it?" "Yes," replied Bridger. "Well, after you get out of the hills on the right hand fork there is scrubby box elders about three miles along the creek up to where a little right hand spring branch puts in with lots and slivers of plum trees about the mouth of it and some old beaver dams at the mouth of the main creek. Well, sir, we went up there and set yesterday morning. I set two traps right below the mouth of that little branch and in them old dams, and Dave set his down the creek apiece. So after we had got our traps set we cruised around and eat plums a while. The best plums I ever saw are there. The trees are loaded and breaking down to the ground with the finest kind, as large as pheasant eggs and sweet as sugar. They'll almost melt in yo' mouth; no wonder them rascally savages like that place so well. Well, sir, after we had eat what plums we wanted, me and Dave took down the creek and stayed all night on a little branch in the hills, and this morning started to our traps. We came up to Dave's traps and in the first there was a four-year-old 'spade,' the next was false licked, went to the next and it had cut a foot and none of the rest disturbed. We then went up to mine to the mouth of the branch. I rode on five or six steps ahead of Dave and just as I got opposite the first trap I heard a rustling in the bushes within about five steps of me. I looked around and pop, pop, pop went the guns, covering me with smoke so close that I could see the blanket wads coming out of the muzzle. Well, sir, I wheeled and a ball hit Too Shebit in the neck and just touched the bone and we pitched heels over head, but Too Shebit raised runnin' and I on his back and the savages jist squattin' and grabbin' at me, but I raised a fog for about half a mile till I overtook Dave."

The foregoing story was corroborated by "Dave," a small, inoffensive man, who had come to the Rocky Mountains with General Ashley some fifteen years before and remained ever since, an excellent hunter and a good trapper. The next day we moved down the stream to its junction with Clark's Fork, within about three miles of the Yellowstone. On the following morning two men went to set traps down on the river and as they were hunting along the brushy banks for places to set, a party of sixty Blackfeet surrounded them, drove them into the river and shot after them as they were swimming across on their horses. One by the name of Howell was shot by two fusee balls through the chest, the other escaped unhurt. Howell rode within half a mile of the camp, fell, and was brought in on a litter. He lived about twenty hours and expired in the greatest agony imaginable. About an hour after he was brought in twenty whites and Delawares went to scour the brush along the river and fight the Blackfeet. Having found them they drove them on to an island and fought them until dark. The loss on our side during the battle was a Nez Perce Indian killed and one white slightly wounded in the shoulder. The Blackfeet, who were fortified on the island, drew off in the night, secreting their dead and carrying off their wounded. The next day we interred the remains of poor Howell at the foot of a large cottonwood tree and called the place "Howell's Encampment," as a compliment to his memory.

11th—We traveled on to Prior's Fork and struck it where the Major's traps were setting, a distance of twenty-five miles southeast. 12th—Stopped at this place and gathered plums. 13th—Traveled east twelve miles to the left hand fork of the Prior. 14th—The snow fell all day and on the 15th it was fifteen inches deep. 16th—We returned to the west fork of the Prior and stopped the next day. 18th—The snow being gone, we returned to Clark's Fork. 19th—Seven of us left the camp and traveled to Rock Fork near the mountain, a distance of thirty-five miles, course southwest. We all kept together and set our traps ran Rocky Fork near the mountain. We had been here five days when a party of Crow Indians came to us, consisting of forty-nine warriors. They were on their way to the Blackfoot village to steal horses. They stayed with us two nights and then went to the camp which had come on to this stream about twenty miles below us.

28th—Another party of Crows came to us, consisting of 110 warriors. We went with them to the camp, which we found about ten miles below. They remained with the camp the next day and then left for the Blackfoot village, which they said was at the three forks of the Missouri, 30th—We traveled with the camp west on to the Rosebud. Oct. 1st—The trappers scattered out in every direction to hunt beaver on the branches of the Rosebud and continued to the 10th, when we followed the camp down the Yellowstone, where Mr. Bridger had concluded to pass the winter. The small streams being frozen, trapping was suspended and all collected to winter quarters, where were thousands of fat buffalo feeding in the plains, and we had nothing to do but slay and eat. Oct. 25—The weather becoming fine and warm, some of the trappers started again to hunt beaver. Myself and another started to Prior's Fork and set our traps on the east branch, where we stayed six days. We then crossed a broken piece of country about twelve miles northeast and fell on to a stream running northeast into the Big Horn, called "Bovy's Fork." Here we set traps and stayed ten days. This section of country was very uneven and broken, but abounded with buffalo, elk, deer, and bear. Among other spontaneous productions of this country were hops, which grew in great abundance and of a superior quality. Thousands of acres along the small branches, the trees and shrubbery were completely entangled in the vines. 11th—The weather becoming cold, the streams froze over again, and we started for camp, which we found on Clark's Fork about a mile above "Howell's Encampment." The camp stopped at this place until Christmas, then moved down about four miles on to the Yellowstone. The bottoms along these rivers were heavily timbered with sweet cottonwood, and our horses and mules were very fond of the bark, which we stripped from the limbs and gave them every night, as the buffalo had entirely destroyed the grass throughout this part of the country. We passed away the time very agreeably, our only employment being to feed our horses, kill buffalo and eat, that is to say, the trappers. The camp keepers' business in winter quarters is to guard the horses, cook and keep fires. We all had snug lodges made of dressed buffalo skins, in the center of which we built a fire and generally comprised about six men to the lodge. The long winter evenings were passed away by collecting in some of the most spacious lodges and entering into debates, arguments or spinning long yarns until midnight, in perfect good humor, and I for one will cheerfully confess that I have derived no little benefit from the frequent arguments and debates held in what we termed "The Rocky Mountain College," and I doubt not but some of my comrades who considered themselves classical scholars have had some little added to their wisdom in the assemblies, however rude they might appear.

On the 28th of January myself and six more trappers concluded to take a cruise of five or six days after buffalo. The snow was about four inches deep and the weather clear and cold. We took seven loose animals to pack meat, and traveled up Clark's Fork about twelve miles, killed a cow and encamped. The next morning we started across toward Rock Fork and had gone about three miles over the smooth plain, gradually ascending to a range of hills which divided Clark's Fork from Rock, when, riding carelessy along with our rifles lying before us on the saddles, we came to a deep, narrow gulch, made by the water running from the hills in the spring season. Behold, the earth seemed teeming with naked savages. A quick volley of fusees, a shower of balls and a cloud of smoke clearly bespoke their nation, tribe, manners and customs, and mode of warfare. A ball broke the right arm of one man and he dropped his rifle, which a savage immediately caught up and shot after us as we wheeled and scampered away out of reach of their guns. There were about eighty Indians, who had secreted themselves until we rode within fifteen feet of them. They got a rifle clear gain, and we had one man wounded and lost a rifle, so they had so much the advantage, and we were obliged to go to camp and study out some plan to get even, as by the two or three skirmishes we had fallen in their respect.

A few days afterwards a party of twenty were discovered crossing the plain to the river about six miles below us. Twenty men immediately mounted and set off and arrived at the place just as they had entered the timber. They ran into some old rotten Indian forts formed of small poles in a conical shape. The whites immediately surrounded and opened fire on them, which was kept up until darkness and the severity of the weather compelled them to retire. We had one man wounded slightly through the hip and one Delaware was shot in the leg by a poisoned ball which lodged under the knee cap. He lived four days and expired. On examining the battleground next day, we found that three or four at least had been killed and put under the ice in the river. Seven or eight had been badly wounded, which they dragged away on trains to their village. We found that the old forts were not bullet proof in any place. Our rifle balls had whistled through them nearly every shot and blood and brains lay scattered about inside on the shattered fragments of the rotten wood.

CHAPTER XIII

Brilliant Display of "Northern Lights" Probably Averts Annihilation of the Camp by Indians

February 22d—Mr. Bridger, according to his usual custom, took his telescope and mounted a high bluff near the encampment to look out for "squalls," as he termed it. About one o'clock PM he returned appearing somewhat alarmed, and on being asked the cause he said the great plain below was alive with savages, who were coming across the hills to the timber about ten miles below us. From this place the river runs in a northeasterly direction, bearing east. On the north and west is a plain from six to ten miles wide, bordered by rough, broken hills and clay bluffs. On the south and east the river runs along the foot of a high range of steep bluffs, intersected by deep ravines and gulches. Along the river are large bottoms covered with large cottonwood timber and clear of underbrush. All hands commenced to build a breast works around the camp, which was constructed of logs and brush piled horizontally six feet high around the camp, inclosing about 250 feet square.

This being completed, at dark a double guard was mounted and all remained quiet, but it was a bitter cold night. I mounted guard from nine till twelve o'clock. The weather was clear, the stars shone with an unusual lustre and the trees cracked like pistols. At about ten o'clock the northern lights commenced streaming up, darting, flashing, rushing to and fro like the movements of an army. At length the shooting and flashing died away and gradually turned to a deep blood red, spreading over one-half the sky. This awful and sublime phenomenon (if I may be allowed to mingle such terms) lasted nearly two hours, then gradually disappeared, and being relieved by the morning guard, I went to bed and slept soundly till sunrise. The next day we were engaged strengthening the fortress by cutting timber from twelve to eighteen inches in diameter, standing them inside on end, leaning them on the breastwork close together. This was completed about noon. About two o'clock Mr. Bridger and six men mounted and went to reconnoiter the enemy, but returned soon after with the intelligence that they were encamped about three miles below on the river and that there was a multitude of them on foot. 24th—The night passed without any disturbance and we began to fear we should not have a fight after all our trouble. About sunrise one solitary savage crept up behind the trees and shot about 200 yards at Mr. Bridger's cook as he was gathering wood outside the fort, then scampered off without doing any damage.

A Spaniard was ordered on to the bluff to look out, and found an Indian in the observatory built on the top, who waited until the Spaniard approached. The Indian then raised and the Spaniard wheeled and took to his heels. The Indian shot and the ball struck him in the heel as he made a fifty-foot leap down the bluff and slid down the snow to the bottom. In about half an hour the word was passed that they were coming on the ice, and presently they appeared coming round a bend of the river in close columns within 400 yards. They then turned off to the right into the plain and called a halt. The chief, who wore a white blanket, came forward a few steps and gave us the signal that he should not fight, but return to his village. They then turned and took a northwest course across the plain toward the three forks of the Missouri. We came to the conclusion after numerous conjectures, that the wonderful appearance of the heavens a few nights previous, connected with our strong fortification, had caused them to abandon the ground without an attack, which is very probable, as all Indians are very superstitious. We supposed, on examining their camp next day, that their numbers must have been about eleven hundred, who had started from their village with the determination of rubbing us from the face of the earth, but that the Great Spirit had shown them that their side of the heavens was bloody, while ours was clear and serene.

February 28th we left our winter quarters on the Yellowstone and started for the Big Horn, the snow being six inches deep on an average. We traveled slowly and reached it in eight days at the mouth of Bovy Fork, about fifteen miles below the lower Big Horn mountain, and then began to slay and eat, but we slayed so much faster than we ate that our meat scaffolds groaned under the weight of fat buffalo meat. We remained here amusing ourselves with playing ball, hopping, wrestling, running foot races, etc., until the 14th of March, when we discovered the Crow village moving down the Big Horn toward us. Immediately all sports were ended. Some mounted horses to meet them, others fortified camp, ready for battle in case there should be a misunderstanding between us. The scouting party soon returned with some of the chiefs, accompanied by an American who was trading with them, in the employ of the American Fur Company. The chiefs, after smoking and looking about for same time, returned to their village, which had encamped about three miles above on the river. The next morning they came and encamped within 300 yards of us. Their village contained 200 lodges and about 200 warriors. The Crows are a proud, haughty, insolent tribe, whenever their party is the strongest, but if the case is reversed they are equally cowardly and submissive. This village was called "Long Hair's" band, after their chief, whose hair was eleven feet six inches long, done up in an enormous queue about eighteen inches long and six inches thick, hanging down his back. He was about eighty years of age and seemed to be afflicted with the dropsy, the only case of the kind I ever knew among the mountain Indians. The village stayed with us until the 25th of March and then moved down the river about six miles.

We left the Big Horn on the 1st of April and started on the spring hunt. On the 3d up Bovy's Fork twenty miles. 4th—Up the same ten miles. After we had encamped four Delawares who were cruising about in the hills hunting buffalo, fell in with a party of ten or twelve Blackfeet, killed one on the spot and wounded several more. The Blackfeet then took to their heels and left the victorious Delawares without loss except one horse being slightly wounded in the neck. 10th—We arrived at "Howell's Encampment" at the mouth of Rocky Fork. The whole country here was filled with buffaloes, driven this way by the Crow village. 11th—We raised a cache of beaver and other articles which had been deposited in the ground in November previous. 14th—A party of twelve trappers and two camp keepers started to trap the "Mussel Shell" River, which heads in the mountain near "Twenty-five Yard" River, and runs into the Missouri on the south side above the mouth of the Yellowstone. Myself and three others started up Rocky Fork about twenty miles, but found so much snow and ice that we could not set our traps for beaver. We found a large cave on the southeast side of a perpendicular rock. In this we encamped six days, during which we made great havoc among the buffaloes. On the 23rd the camp moved up to our cave and the next day I went up the stream about twelve miles and set my traps and saw signs of several war parties of Blackfeet who were scouting about the country. 26th—I was cruising with another trapper through the timber and brush above where we had set our traps, when on a sudden we came within ten steps of two Blackfoot forts and saw the smoke ascending from the tops. As we saw no individuals we entered and found the Indians had been gone about half an hour. 28th—The party arrived from the Mussel Shell, having been defeated and lost one trapper and nearly all their horses and traps by the Blackfeet.

May 1st—All being collected, we left Rocky Fork close to the mountain and took around the foot in an easterly direction and encamped at a spring, where we stayed the next day. The Blackfeet still continued dogging at our heels and to steal now and then a horse which might get loose in the night. There is a proverb among the mountaineers that "it is better to count ribs than tracks." That is to say, it is better to fasten a horse at night until you can count his ribs from poverty than turn him loose to fatten and count his tracks after an Indian has stolen him. 3d—Traveled on to Clark's Fork twelve miles southeast, and the next day up the same fifteen miles south. 5th—Traveled to a small branch running into Stinking River, southerly direction fifteen miles. 6th—We encamped on Stinking River about fifteen miles below the forks, distance twelve miles, course southeast. 7th—We traveled from the river about twenty miles in a southerly direction and encamped at a spring. 8th—To the "Gray Bull" Fork of the Big Horn. 9th—To the Medicine Lodge Fork, twelve miles south. 10th—To the middle Fork of the Medicine Lodge, eight miles. 11th—To the South Fork of the Medicine Lodge, eight miles south. Here we stayed two days. 14th—Traveled southeast to a small spring at the foot of the upper Big Horn mountain, distance twelve miles. The 15th traveled to the top of the Big Horn mountain and encamped on the divide. The country over which we had traveled since we left the "Stinking" was much broken by spurs of mountains and deep gullies, entirely destitute of timber except along the banks of the streams. 16th—Traveled down the mountain on the south side and encamped on a small branch of Wind River. This river loses its name whilst passing through the upper Big Horn mountains. From thence it takes the name of the Big Horn, derived from the vast numbers of mountain sheep or big horn inhabiting the mountains through which it passes. 17th—Over broken country south about fifteen miles. 18th—Encamped on the river after a march of ten miles south. 19th—The camp intending to stop here several days, I started with a raw son of Erin to hunt beaver on the headwaters of the river. We traveled up west about twenty-five miles to what was called the "Red Rock." Killed a sheep and encamped for the night where several branches of the river united. 20th—We took up a large branch about fifteen miles northwest, and found the water over-flowing the banks of all the branches so much that it was impossible to catch beaver. We then altered our course northeast across the country in order to examine the small branches on our right, but finding all our efforts to trap useless and discovering that a war party consisting of eighty Blackfeet were in pursuit of us, we returned to the camp by a different route on the 23d. 24th—Traveled with the camp to the North Fork of "Popo-azia" or Pope River, one of the principal branches of Wind River, distance twelve miles. Course south. 25th—To the middle fork of the same stream, eight miles distance. 26th—To the oil spring on the South Fork of Popo-azia. This spring produced about one gallon per hour of pure oil or coal or rather coal tar, the scent of which is often carried on the wind five or six miles. The oil issues from the ground within thirty feet of the stream and runs off slowly into the water. Camp stopped here eight days. We set fire to the spring when there was two or three barrels of oil on the ground about it. It burned very quick and clear, but produced a dense column of thick, black smoke. The oil above ground being consumed, the fire soon went out. This was a beautiful country, thickly clothed with grass, intermingled with Bowers of every hue. On the west rose the Wind River range of mountains abruptly from the smooth, rolling hills, until crowned with snow above the clouds. On the east stretched away the great Wind River plain and terminated at a low range of mountains rising between Wind and Powder Rivers. Buffalo, elk, and sheep were abundant. Beds of iron and coal were frequently found in this part of the country.

June 5th we left the oil spring and took over a point of mountain about fifteen miles southwest and encamped on a small spring branch. 6th—Crossed the spurs of mountains due west twelve miles and encamped on a branch of Sweetwater. 7th—Traveled west about fifteen miles and encamped on "Little Sandy," a branch of Green River. 8th—Traveled north up the valley about eighteen miles and encamped on a stream called the New Fork of Green River where we stayed the next day. 10th—Traveled west to the main river about twenty-five miles, and struck the river about twelve miles below the mouth of Horse Creek.

CHAPTER XIV

Another Rendezvous at Green River—Making "Good Indians"—
The Arrival of Wagon Train and Supplies

Here we found the hunting parties all assembled waiting
for the arrival of supplies from the States. Here presented
what might be termed a mixed multitude. The whites were
chiefly Americans and Canadian French, with some Dutch,
Scotch, Irish, English, halfbreed, and fullblood Indians
of nearly every tribe in the Rocky Mountains. Some were
gambling at cards, some playing the Indian game of "hand"
and others horse racing, while here and there could be seen
small groups collected under shady trees relating the events
of the past year, all in good spirits and health, for sickness
is a stranger seldom met with in these regions. Sheep, elk,
deer, buffalo, and bear skins mostly supply the mountaineers
with clothing, lodges, and bedding, while the meat of the
same animals supply them with food. They have not the
misfortune to get any of the luxuries from the civilized world
but once a year, and then in such small quantities that they
last but a few days.

We had not remained in this quiet manner long before
something new arose for our amusement. The Bannock
Indians had for several years lived with the whites on terms
partly hostile, frequently stealing horses and traps, and in

one instance killed two white trappers. They had taken some horses and traps from a party of French trappers who were hunting Bear River in April previous, and they were now impudent enough to come with the village of sixty lodges and encamp within three miles of us in order to trade with the whites as usual, still having the stolen property in their possession and refusing to give it up. On the 15th of June four or five whites and two Nez Perce Indians went to their village and took the stolen horses (whilst the men were out hunting buffalo) and returned with them to our camp. About three o'clock PM of the same day thirty Bannocks came riding at full gallop up to the camp, armed with their war weapons. They rode into the midst and demanded the horses which the Nez Perces had taken saying they did not wish to fight with the whites. But the Nez Perces, who were only six in number, gave the horses to the whites for protection, which we were bound to give, as they were numbered among our trappers and far from their own tribe. Some of the Bannocks, on seeing this, started to leave the camp. One of them as he passed me observed that he did not come to fight the whites; but another, a fierce looking savage, who still stopped behind, called out to the others, saying, "We came to get our horses or blood and let us do it," I was standing near the speaker and understood what he said. I immediately gave the whites warning to be in readiness for an attack. Nearly all the men in camp were under arms. Mr. Bridger was holding one of the stolen horses by the bridle when one of the Bannocks rushed through the crowd, seized the bridle, and attempted to drag it from Mr. Bridger by force, without heeding the cocked rifles that surrounded him any more than if they had been so many reeds in the hands of children. He was a brave Indian, but his bravery proved fatal to himself, for the moment he seized the bridle two rifle balls whistled through his body. The others wheeled to run, but twelve of them were shot from their horses before they were out of reach of rifle. We then mounted horses and pursued them, destroyed and plundered their village, and followed and fought them three days, when they begged us to let them go and promised to be good Indians in future. We granted their request and returned to our camp, satisfied that the best way to negotiate and settle disputes with hostile Indians is with the rifle, for that is the only pen that can write a treaty which they will not forget. Two days after we left them three white trappers, ignorant of what had taken place, went into their village and were treated in the most friendly manner. The Indians said, however, they had been fighting with the Blackfeet.

July 5th a party arrived from the States with supplies. The cavalcade consisted of forty-five men and twenty carts drawn by mules, under the direction of Mr. Thomas Fitzpatrick, accompanied by Capt. William Stewart on another tour of the Rocky Mountains.

Joy now beamed in every countenance. Some received letters from their friends and relations; some received the public papers and news of the day; others consoled themselves with the idea of getting a blanket, a cotton shirt, or a few pints of coffee and sugar to sweeten it just by way of a treat, gratis, that is to say, by paying 2,000 percent on the first cost by way of accommodation. For instance, sugar, $2 per pint, coffee the same, blankets $20 each, tobacco , $2 per pound, alcohol $4 per pint, and common cotton shirts $5 each, etc. And in return paid $4 or $5 per pound for beaver. In a few days the bustle began to subside. The furs were done up in packs ready for transportation to the States and parties were formed for the hunting the ensuing year. One party, consisting of 110 men, was destined for the Blackfoot country, under the direction of L.B. Fontanelle as commander and James Bridger as pilot. I started, with five others to hunt the headwaters of the Yellowstone, Missouri and Big Hom Rivers, a portion of the country I was particularly fond of hunting.

CHAPTER XV

Back Again to the Hunting Grounds—Solitary Reflections on a Peak of the Rockies

On the 20th of July we left the rendezvous and traveled up Green River about ten miles. 21st—We traveled up Green River until noon, when we discovered a trail of eight or ten Blackfeet and a buffalo fresh killed and butchered, with the meat tied up in small bundles on the ground, which they had left on seeing us approach, and ran into the bushes. We, supposing them to be a small scouting party, tied their bundles of meat on to our saddles and still kept on our route but had not gone far before we discovered them secreted among some willows growing along a branch which crossed our trail. I was ahead leading the party when I discovered them. We stopped and one of my comrades, whose name was Allen, began to arrange the load on his pack mule. In the meantime I reined my horse to the left and rode onto a small hillock nearby and casting a glance towards the bushes, which were about 150 yards distant, I saw two guns pointed at me. I instantly wheeled my horse, but to no purpose. The two balls struck him, one in the loins and the other in the shoulder, which dropped him under me. The Indians at the same time jumped out of the bushes, sixty or seventy in number, and ran toward us, shooting and yelling. I jumped on a horse behind one of my comrades and we scampered away toward the rendezvous, where we arrived at dark. 25th—The parties started and all traveled with Mr. Fontanelle's party up Green River ten miles, intending to keep in their company five or six days and then branch off to our first intended route. 26th—We traveled twenty miles northwest across a low range of hills and encamped in a valley lying on a branch of Lewis Fork called "Jackson's Little Hole." 27th—We traveled down this stream 18 miles northwest. This stream ran through a tremendous mountain in a deep, narrow canyon of rocks. The trail ran along the cliffs from 50 to 200 feet above its bed and was so narrow in many places that only one horse could pass at a time for several hundred yards, and one false step would precipitate one into the chasm below. After leaving the canyon we encamped at a small spring in "Jackson's Big Hole," near the Southern extremity. 28th—Traveled up the valley north fifteen miles and encamped. Killed some buffalo and stayed next day. 30th—Left the camp in company with two trappers and one camp keeper. We received instructions from Mr. Fontanelle to meet the camp at the mouth of Clark's Fork of the Yellowstone on the 15th of the ensuing October, where they expected to pass the winter, but he said if he should conclude to change his winter quarters he would cause a tree to be marked at Howell's grave and bury a letter in the ground at the foot of it containing directions for finding the camp.

We traveled north till near sunset and encamped about forty miles from the main party. 31st—We traveled to the fork five miles below Jackson's Lake and ascended it in the same direction I had done the season before and encamped about fifteen miles from the valley. August 1st—We reached the dividing spring about four o'clock PM and stopped for the night. 2d—We encamped at the inlet of the Yellowstone Lake. 3d—Traveled down the east shore of the lake and stopped for the night near the outlet at the steam springs. 4th—We took our course east northeast and after traveling all day over rugged mountains, thickly covered with pines and underbrush, we encamped at night about ten miles north of the secluded valley, on the stream which runs through it. After we had encamped we killed a deer, which came in good time, as we had eaten the last of our provisions the night previous at the Yellowstone Lake and the flies and mosquitoes were so bad and the underbrush so thick that we had not killed anything during the day. 5th—We traveled up a left hand branch of this stream northeast fifteen miles through the thick pines and brush until near the head, where we encamped in a beautiful valley about two miles in circumference, almost encircled with huge mountains whose tops were covered with snow, from which small rivulets were issuing clear as crystal, and, uniting in the smooth, grassy vale, formed the stream which we had ascended. We concluded to spend the next day at this place, as there were no flies or mosquitoes, for though warm and pleasant in the day, the nights were too cold for them to survive. The next day, after eating a light breakfast of roasted venison, I shouldered my rifle and ascended the highest mountain on foot. I reached the snow in about an hour, when, seating myself upon a huge fragment of granite and having full view of the country around me in a few moments was almost lost in contemplation. This, said I, is not a place where heroes' deeds of chivalry have been achieved in days of yore, neither is it a place of which bards have sung until the world knows the precise posture of every rock and tree or the winding turn of every streamlet. But on the contrary those stupendous rocks whose surface is formed into irregular benches rising one above another from the vale to the snow, dotted here and there with low pines and covered with green herbage intermingled with flowers, with the scattered flocks of sheep and elk carelessly feeding or thoughtlessly reposing beneath the shade, having Providence for their founder and Nature for shepherd, gardener, and historian. In viewing scenes like this the imagination of one unskilled in science wanders to the days of the Patriarchs and after numerous conjecturing returns without any fixed decision. Wonder is put to the test, but having no proof for its argument, a doubt still remains, but supposition steps forward and taking the place of knowledge, in a few words solves the mysteries of ages, centuries and eras. After indulging in such a train of reflections for about two hours, I descended to the camp, where I found my companions had killed a fat buck elk during my absence and some of the choicest parts of it were supported on sticks around the fire. My ramble had sharpened my appetite and the delicious flavor of roasted meat soon rid my brain of romantic ideas. My companions were men who never troubled themselves about vain and frivolous notions, as they called them. With them every country was pretty when there was weather, and as to beauty of nature or arts it was all a "humbug," as one of them, an Englishman, often expressed it. "Talk of a fine country," said he, "and beautiful places in these mountains. If you want to see a beautiful place, go to Highland and see the Duke of Rutland's place." "Aye" says a son of Erin, who sat opposite with an elk rib in one hand and a butcher knife in the other, while the sweat rolling from his face mingled in the channels of grease which ran from the corners of his mouth, "Aye, an' ye would see a pretty place, go to old Ireland and take a walk in Lord Farnham's domain. That is the place where ye can see plisure. Arrah, an' if I were upon that same ground this day I'd fill my body with good old whisky." "Yes," says the backwoods hunter on my left, as he cast away his bone and smoothed down his long auburn hair with his greasy hand, "Yes, you English and Irish are always talking about your fine countries, but if they are so mighty fine," said he with an oath, "why do so many of you run off and leave them and come to America to get a living?" From this the conversation turned into an argument in which the hunter came off victorious, driving his opponents from the field.

CHAPTER XVI

Thieving Indians steal Most of the Horses—A "Whistling" Elk Scares the Tenderfoot Camptender

Aug. 7th—We traveled up the mountain in a southerly direction and fell into a smooth, grassy defile about 200 paces wide, which led through between two high peaks of rock. In this place we fell in with a large band of sheep, killed two ewes, packed the best meat on our horses and proceeded down the defile, which led us on to the head waters of "Stinking" River, about fifty miles from where it enters the plain. We traveled down the stream about ten miles south and encamped where we saw some signs of Snake Indians who inhabited these wilds. The next morning I arose about daybreak and went in search of our horses, which had been turned loose to feed during the night. I soon found all but three, and after hunting some time I discovered a trail made in the dew on the grass where an Indian had been crawling on his belly, and soon found where he had caught the horses. Two of us then mounted mules and followed the trail in a westerly direction up a steep, piney mountain until about ten o'clock, when we lost the trail among the rocks and were obliged to give up the pursuit. We then returned to camp and packed our remaining animals and traveled down the stream about ten miles. 9th—We left the main stream and ascended a small branch in a south southwest direction about eight miles, up a steep ascent, and encamped in a smooth, grassy spot near the head, where we concluded to stop the next day and hunt beaver. Early the next morning a few of the "Mountain Snakes" came to our camp, consisting of three men and five or six women and children. One of them told me he knew the Indians who had stolen our horses; that they lived in the mountains between Stinking River and Clark's Fork, and said that he would try to get them. After trading some beaver and sheep skins from them, talking, smoking, etc., about an hour, I mounted my mule with six traps and my rifle, and one of my comrades did the same, and we started to hunt beaver. We left the camp in a southwest direction and traveled about eight miles over a high, craggy mountain, then descended into a small circular valley about a mile in circumference, which was completely covered with logs, shattered fragments of trees and splinters four or five feet deep. There had been trees two and three feet in diameter broken off within two feet of the ground and shivered into pieces small enough for a kitchen fireplace. This, in an probability, was the effect of an avalanche about two years previous, as the tall pines had been completely cleared for the space of 400 yards wide and more than two miles up the side of the mountain. Finding no beaver on the branches of this stream, we returned to camp at sunset. Our camp keeper had prepared an excellent supper of grizzly bear meat and mutton, nicely stewed and seasoned with salt and pepper, which, as the mountain saying goes, is not bad to take upon an empty stomach after a hard day's riding and climbing

over the mountains and rocks. Aug. 11th—We returned to
the river and traveled up about four miles, then left it and
traveled up a branch in a due east direction about six miles,
killed a couple of fat doe elk and encamped. 12th—Myself
and Allen (which was the name of the backwoodsman)
started to hunt the small streams in the mountains to the
west of us, leaving the Englishman, who was the other trapper, to set traps about the camp. We hunted the branches
of this stream, then crossed the divide to the waters of the
Yellowstone Lake, where we found the whole country swarming with elk. We killed a fat buck for supper and encamped for the night. The next day Allen shot a grizzly bear and
bursted the percussion tube of his rifle, which obliged us to
return to our comrades on the 13th and make another tube.
The next day we returned to Stinking River and traveled up
about ten miles above where we first struck it. 15th—It rained
and snowed all day and we stopped in camp. 16th—Took
a northeast course up the mountain and reached the divide
about noon, then descended in a direction nearly east and
encamped in a valley on the head of Clark's Fork. This valley
is a prairie about thirty miles in circumference, completely
surrounded by high mountains. The stream, after passing
southeast, falls into a tremendous canyon just wide enough to
admit its waters between rocks from 300 to 500 feet perpendicular height, extending about twelve miles to the great plain.
18th—We moved up the stream to the head of the valley and
encamped. Here the stream is formed of two forks nearly
equal in size. The right hand fork falls into the left from off

a bench upwards of 700 feet high, nearly perpendicular. The view of it at a distance of eight or ten miles resembles a bank of snow. 19th—Traveled up the west branch about ten miles northwest through thick pines and fallen timber, then leaving the stream to our right turned into a defile which led us on to the waters of the Yellowstone in about eight miles, where we stopped, set traps for beaver, and stayed next day. 21st—We traveled down this stream, which runs west through a high range of mountains about twenty-five miles. 22d—Traveled down the stream about fifteen miles west and encamped in the secluded valley, where we stayed two days. 25th—Traveled down the valley to the north and crossed a low space about four miles north and fell on to a stream running into the one we had left. Here we set traps and stayed until the 2d of September. 3d—Traveled over a high, rugged mountain about twenty miles northwest and camped in a beautiful valley on a small stream running into the one we had left in the morning. 4th—Traveled fifteen miles northwest over a high, piney mountain and encamped on a stream running south into the Yellowstone, where we stayed and trapped until the 13th. We then traveled up the stream northeast about eight miles. 14th—Traveled up the stream twelve miles in the same direction. 15th—We crossed the divide of the main range north towards the Big Plains. We found the snow belly deep to our horses. After leaving the snow we traveled about eight miles north and encamped on the head branch of the cross creek running north into the Yellowstone about twelve miles below the mouth of "Twenty-five Yard" River.

Here a circumstance occurred which furnished the subject for a good joke upon our green Irish camp keeper. The Englishman had stopped on the mountain to hunt sheep, while we descended to the stream and encamped on a prairie about two miles in circumference. It was the commencement of the rutting season with the elk, when the bucks frequently utter a loud cry resembling a shrill whistle, especially when they see anything of a strange appearance. We had made our beds at night on a little bench between two small, dry gullies. The weather was clear and the moon shone brightly. About ten o'clock at night, when I supposed my comrades fast asleep, an elk blew his shrill whistle within about 100 yards of us. I took my gun, slipped silently into the gully and crept toward the place where I heard the sound, but I soon found he had been frightened by the horses and ran off up the mountain. On turning back I met Allen, who, hearing the elk, had started to get a shot at him in the same manner I had done without speaking a word. We went back to camp, but our camp keeper was nowhere to be found. We searched the bushes high and low, ever and anon calling for "Conn," but no "Conn" answered. At length Allen, cruising through the brush, tumbled over a pile of rubbish, when lo! Conn was beneath, nearly frightened out of his wits. "Arrah! an' is it you, Allen?" said he trembling as if an ague fit was shaking him. "But I thought the whole world was full of the spalpeens of savages. And where are they gone?" It was near an hour before we could satisfy him of his mistake, and I dare say his slumbers were by no means soft or smooth during the remainder of the night.

CHAPTER XVII

Main Party Fails to Keep Appointment at "Howell's Encampment"—
Stampeded Buffalo

16th—The Englishman arrived and we traveled down this stream about ten miles, where we stayed the next day, as it snowed very hard. 18th—Traveled down about twenty miles and on the 19th came to the plains in about ten miles travel, where we encamped. Here we found the country filled with buffalo as usual. 20th—We shaped our course northeast and traveled about twenty-five miles across the spurs of the mountain, fell on to the north fork of the Rosebud, where we stayed the next day, as it rained. 22d—We traveled south along the foot of the mountain for twenty miles, keeping among the low spurs which project into the plain, in order to prevent being discovered by any straggling parties of Blackfeet which might chance to be lurking about the country. The plains below us were crowded with buffalo, which we were careful not to disturb for fear of being discovered. We stopped and set our traps on the small branches of the Rosebud until the 11th of October, then traveled to Rocky Fork and went up it into the mountains and encamped. On the 13th myself and Allen started to hunt Mr. Fontanell's party, leaving our comrades in the mountains to await our return. We traveled down Rocky Fork all day amid crowds of buffalo and encamped after dark near the mouth. The next morning we went to "Howell's Encampment," but found no tree marked, neither had the earth been disturbed since we had closed it upon the remains of the unfortunate Howell. We now sat down and consulted upon the best course to pursue. As winter was approaching we could not think of stopping in this country, where parties of Blackfeet were ranging at all seasons of the year. After a few moments' deliberation, we came to the conclusion, and I wrote a note, enclosed it in a buffalo horn, buried it at the foot of the tree, and then marked the tree with my hatchet. This being done we mounted our mules and started back to the mountains. We traveled about six miles and then stopped and killed a cow. As we were lying within about sixty paces of the band, which contained about 300 cows, Allen made an observation which I shall never forget. Said he, "I have been watching those cows some time and I can see but one that is poor enough to kill, for," said he, "it is a shame to kill one of those large, fat cows merely for two men's supper." So saying he leveled his rifle on the poorest and brought her down. She was a heifer about three years old and but an inch of fat on her back. After cooking and eating we proceeded on our journey until some time after dark, when we found ourselves on a sudden in the midst of an immense band of buffaloes, which, getting the scent of us, ran helter-skelter around us in every direction, rushing to and fro like the waves of the ocean, approaching sometimes within ten feet of us. We stood still, for we dared not retreat or advance until this stream of brutes took a general course and rolled away like distant thunder, and then we hurried on through Egyptian darkness a few hundred paces, where we found a bunch of willows and concluded to stop for the night rather than risk our lives any further among such a whirlwind of beef. 15th—We reached the camp about ten o'clock AM. We stayed on Rocky Fork and its branches trapping until the 27th of October, when we concluded to go to a small fork running into Wind River on the east side above the upper Big Horn mountain, and there pass the winter unless we should hear from the main party. 28th—We traveled to Clark's Fork and the next day to Stinking River, east southeast direction. 30th—We crossed Stinking River and traveled in the same direction over a broken, barren tract of country about thirty-five miles, whilst the rain poured all day in torrents. About sun an hour high we stopped and the weather cleared up. We encamped for the night in a small ravine, where some water was standing in a puddle, but there was no wood save a lone green cottonwood tree which had supported a bald eagle's nest probably more than half a century. 31st—We traveled over ground similar to that of the day before, shaping our course more easterly until night. Nov. 1st—After traveling about ten miles we reached the Big Horn River and stopped and commenced setting traps. The river at this place was bordered with heavy cottonwood timber with little or no brush beneath.

CHAPTER XVIII

Threatened and Robbed by the Crow Indians, the Hunters Proceed Afoot to Fort William, Enduring Great Hardship

Along towards night a party of Crow Indians came to us on foot, armed as if going to war. After smoking and eating they told us they were on their way to the Snakes to steal horses and intended to stay all night with us and leave the next morning. They told us the village to which they belonged was nearly a day's travel below on the river and that Long Hair's village was on Wind River above the mountain, but could give us no information of Mr. Fontanell or his party. They were very insolent and saucy, saying we had no right in their country, and intimated they could take everything from us if they wished. The next morning after eating breakfast they said if we would give them some tobacco and ammunition they would leave us, so we divided our little stock with them. They then persisted in having all, and when we refused them, telling them we could not spare it, one of them seized the sack which contained it, while another grasped the Englishman's rifle. We immediately wrenched them out of their hands and told them if they got more they should fight for it. During the scuffle they had all presented their arms, but when we gained possession of the rifle and the sack, they put down their arms and told us, with an envious savage laugh, they were only joking, but we were too well acquainted with the Crows to relish such capers as mere jokes and wished to get out of their power the easiest way possible, as their villages were on either side of us. We then packed up our horses and forded the river and traveled up about six miles and encamped. At the same time the Indians were mounted on our pack horses and riding animals trailing us and the remainder on foot, except one who returned towards the village crying. After we had stopped they made a sort of shelter, as it looked likely for rain, and at night ordered us to go into it and sleep, but we bluntly refused and removed our baggage about thirty paces from them. Sitting down reclining against it, one of them had taken the only blanket I possessed off my riding saddle and put an old worn out coat in its place, with a hint that exchanging was not robbing. They laid down in their shelter and continued to sing their noisy and uncouth war songs until near midnight, when they ceased and all became silent. The night was dark with a sprinkling of rain. We lay without hearing any disturbance until daybreak, when we began to look around, but could find neither Indians nor horses, though we soon found their trail going down the river. We then set about burning our saddles, robes, etc., and caching our beaver in the ground, intending after making a few deposits and bon fires to shoulder our rifles and travel to Fort William at the mouth of Savorney's Fork of the Platte.

Our saddles, epishemores, ropes, etc., were scarcely consumed when we saw five or six Indians on horseback coming
toward us at full gallop and presently fifteen or twenty
more appeared following them. They rode up, alighted
from their horses and asked for tobacco to smoke. We gave
then some. They formed a circle and sat down. I was not
acquainted with any of them except the chief, who was called the "Little Soldier." He spoke to me in the Snake language and said he wished me to smoke with them, but the
manner in which they had formed the ring and placed
their war weapons excited suspicion, and Allen immediately declined, as he had lived with the Crows two winters
and said he knew that thieving and treachery were two of
the greatest virtues the nation could boast of, and we
quickly resolved to leave them at all hazards. So we shouldered our rifles and those who had blankets took them
and began to travel. The Indians looked at us with preten-
ded astonishment and asked what was the matter. Allen
told them that he was aware that they wanted to rob us
and were laying plans to do it without danger to themselves, but, said he, "if you follow us or molest us we will
besmear the ground with blood and guts of Crow Indians,
and do not speak to me more," said he, "for I despise the
odious jargon of your nation." So saying he wheeled around
and we marched away in a southerly direction toward the
mountain. We had not gone far before two of them came
after us. We stopped and turned round, when one of them
stopped within 300 paces of us, while the other, who was

the chief, advanced slowly unarmed. When he came up he addressed me in the Snake language, for knowing the disposition of Allen, he did not wish to trifle with his own life so much as to begin a conversation with him in his own language. Taking me by the hand as he spoke, he said, "My friends, you are very foolish. You do not know how bad my heart feels to think that you have been robbed by men belonging to my village; but they are not men, they are dogs who took your animals. The first I knew of your being in this country, about midnight a young man came to the village crying and told me of their intention. I immediately mounted my horse and hastened to your assistance, but arrived too late, but if you will go with me I will get your animals and give you some saddles and robes and fit you out as well as I can. You can then stay with me until the blanket chief comes" (the name they gave Mr. Bridger). I interpreted what he had said to my comrades, but they said tell him we will not go to the Crow village; we will not trust our lives among them. When I told him this, he replied, "I am very sorry. What shall I say to the blanket chief? How can I hold up my head when I shall meet him, and what shall I do with the things you have left behind?" I told him to give them to the blanket chief. He then turned and left us, slowly and sadly, but I am well aware that a Crow Indian can express great sorrow for me and at the same time be laying a plan to rob me or secretly take my life. After he had left us we traveled on towards the mountains about ten miles, stopped, killed a cow, and ate supper, and then traveled until about midnight, when, it being dark and cloudy, we stopped and kindled a fire with sage and weeds which we gathered about us, and sat down to wait for daylight. Sleep was far from us. Our minds were so absorbed in the reflections on the past that few were the words that passed among us during the night. A short time after we stopped it commenced snowing very fast and we were obliged to hover over our little fire to keep it from being extinguished. The day at length appeared and we proceeded on our journey toward the mountains, while it still continued to snow. As we began to ascend the mountain the snow grew deeper, and about noon was up to our knees. We traveled on until sun about an hour high, and stopped at some scrubby cedars and willows which grew around a spring. After scraping away the snow we built a fire, broke some cedar boughs, spread them on the ground and laid down, weary and hungry, but we had meat enough with us for supper. Three of us, myself, Allen and Greenberry, had been more or less inured to the hardships of a hunter's life, but our camp keeper, John Conn, could not relish the manner in which he was treated in a country that boasted so much of its freedom and independence, and often wished himself back on the shamrock shore. Myself and Allen had one blanket between us, the others had a blanket each. The wind blew cold and the snow drifted along the brow of the mountains around us. When we arose in the morning our fire had gone out, the snow was three inches deep on our covering, and it still kept snowing.

Allen killed a black-tailed deer close by and we concluded to stop all day at this place. Nov. 6th—The sun rose clear and we started up the mountain, keeping on the ridges where the wind had driven off the snow, and arrived at the top about ten o'clock AM. From this elevation we could see the Wind River plains, which were dry and dusty, whilst we were in snow up to the middle. We killed some sheep which were in large numbers about us, cooked some of the best meat over a slow fire, packed it on our backs and proceeded down the mountain south and slept on bare ground that night. Nov. 7th—We arose and found ourselves much refreshed by our night's rest. We traveled nearly east all day, ascending a gradual smooth slope of country which lies between Wind and Powder Rivers, and stopped at night on the divide, where we found the snow hard and about two inches deep and the weather cold and windy, whilst not a stick of wood or a drop of water were to be found within ten miles of us. We found a place washed out by the water in the spring of the year. It was the only shelter to be had, and digging down to the dry earth, scattered some branches of sage upon it to lie upon. I then went in search of a rock in order to heat it and melt snow in my hat, but I could not find so much as a pebble, so we kindled a little fire of sage and sat down with a piece of mutton in one hand and a piece of snow in the other. Eating meat and snow in this manner we made out our supper and laid down to shake, tremble, and suffer with the cold till daylight, when we started and traveled as fast as our wearied limbs would permit in the same direction we had traveled the day before, descending a gradual slope toward the head of Powder River, until near night, when finding some water standing in a puddle, with large quantities of sage about it, we killed a bull nearby, and taking his skin for a bed and some of the best meat for supper, we passed the night very comfortably. We were now in sight of the red buttes on the River Platte, which appeared about forty miles distant southeast.

The next morning we found the weather foggy, with sleet and snow falling. I tried to persuade my comrades to stop until it should clear away, urging the probability of our steering a wrong course, as we could not see more than 200 paces, but they concluded we could travel by the wind, and after making several objections to traveling by such an uncertain guide to no purpose, I gave up the argument and we started and traveled about east southeast for three hours as we supposed, then stopped a short time and built a fire of sage, while it continued to rain and snow alternately, and seeing no signs of the weather clearing, we started again and went on until near night, when, the sun coming out, we found that instead of traveling south southeast our course had been north northeast and we were as far from the Platte as we were in the morning, with the country around us very broken and intersected with deep ravines and gullies. We saw some bulls three or four miles ahead and we started for them. After the sun had set it clouded up and began to rain. We reached the bulls about an hour after dark. Allen crawled close to them, shot and killed one, took off the skin and some of the meat, whilst myself and the others were groping about in the dark hunting a few bits of sage and weeds to make a fire, and after repeated unsuccessful exertions we at last kindled a blaze. We had plenty of water under, over, and all around us, but could not find a stick for fuel bigger than a man's thumb. We sat down around the fire with each holding a piece of beef over it on a stick with one hand while the other was employed in keeping up the blaze by feeding it with sage and weeds until the meat was warmed through, when it was devoured, with an observation that "bull meat was dry eating when cooked too much." After supper (if I may be allowed to disgrace the term by applying it to such a wolfish feast) we spread the bull skin down in the mud in the dryest place we could find, and laid down upon it. Our fire was immediately put out by the rain and all was Egyptian darkness. We lay tolerably comfortable while the skin retained its animal warmth and remained above the surface, but the mud being soft, the weight of our bodies sunk it by degrees below the water level, which ran under us on the skin. We concluded it was best to lie still and keep the water that was about us warm, for if we stirred we let in the cold water and if we moved our bed we were more likely to find a worse, instead of a better, place, as it rained hard all night. At daylight we arose, bid adieu to our uncomfortable lodgings, and left as fast as our legs would carry us through the mud and water, and after traveling about twelve miles

south course, we stopped, killed a bull, and took breakfast. After eating, we traveled south until sunset. The weather was clear and cold, but we found plenty of dry sage to
make a fire and dry weeds for a bed. 11th—The ground was
frozen hard in the moming and the wind blew cold from
the north. We traveled until about noon, when we fell in
with large bands of buffalo, and seeing the red buttes about
five or six miles ahead we killed two fat cows and took as
much of the meat as we could conveniently carry and traveled to the Platte, where we arrived about the middle of
the afternoon, weary and fatigued. Here we had plenty of
wood, water, meat, and dry grass to sleep on, and taking
everything into consideration, we thought ourselves comfortably situated—comfortably, I say, for mountaineers, not
for those who never repose on anything but a bed of down
or sit or recline on anything harder than silken cushions,
for such would spurn the idea of a hunter talking about
comfort and happiness. But experience is the best teacher,
hunger good sauce, and I really think to be acquainted
with misery contributes to the enjoyment of happiness, and
to know one's self greatly facilitates the knowledge of man-
kind. One thing I often console myself with, and that is,
the earth will lie as hard upon the monarch as it will upon
the hunter, and I have no assurance that it will lie upon me
at all. My bones may, in a few years, or perhaps days, be
bleaching upon the plains in these regions, like many of my
occupation, without a friend to turn even a turf upon them
after a hungry wolf has finished his feast.

CHAPTER XIX

Fort William—A Cool Reception—Sioux Sign Language—Three Miles of Deer in One Band

12th—The sun rose clear and warm and we found ourselves much refreshed by our night's rest. We traveled down the river about five miles, waded across it, and stopped the remainder of the day. I had a severe attack of rheumatism in my knees and ankles, but this was no place to be sick, so we jogged along over the Black Hills, having plenty of wood, water, and fresh buffalo meat every night, until the 18th, when we reached Fort William. When I entered this fort I was met by two of my old messmates, who invited me to their apartments. I now felt myself at home, as Mr. Fontanell was one of the chief proprietors of the establishment, and who had been partly, and I may say wholly, the cause of our misfortunes. At night I lay down, but the pains in my legs and feet drove sleep from me. The next day I walked around the fort as well as I could in order to get my joints limber, and on the third day after our arrival I felt quite recovered and at breakfast I asked my messmates where the man was who had charge of the fort. They replied he was in his house, pointing across the square. I inquired if he was sick, for I had not seen him. They said he was unwell, but not so

as to confine him to his room. I observed I must go and see
him, as I discovered he was not coming to see me, so saying,
Allen and myself started across the square and met him on
the way from the storehouse to his dwelling room. We bid
him "good morning," which he coldly returned and was on
the point of turning carelessly away, when we told him we
would like to get some robes for bedding, likewise a shirt or
two and some other necessary articles. "Well," said he, "as
for blankets, shirts or coats, I have none, and Mr. Fontanell
has left no word when there will be any come up." "If that is
the case," I replied, "you can let us have some buffalo robes
and epishemores." "Yes," said he, "I believe I can let you have
an epishemore or two. Here, John, go up into yonder bastion and show these men those epishemores that were put
up there some time ago." "I don't think there are any there,"
replied John, "but some old ones, and them the rats have
cut all to pieces." "Oh, I guess you can find some there that
will do," he replied, turning around and swinging a key on
his thumb as the insignia of his dignified position and with
a stiff stride walked to his apartments, while we followed
the Major Domo of this elevated quadruped to the bastion,
where I took the best epishemore I could find, which was
composed of nine pieces of buffalo skin sewed together. But
necessity compelled me to take it, knowing at the same time
there were more than 500 new robes in the warehouse which
did not cost a pint of whisky each. But they were for the
people in the U. S. and not for trappers. This was the 21st
day of November, 1837. I never shall forget the time, place

nor circumstance, but shall always pity the being who held imperial sway over a few sticks of wood, with five or six men to guard them. It was not his fault, for how should he depart from the way in which he had been brought up? And what is more, trappers have no right to meet with bad luck, for it is nothing more nor less than the result of bad management. This is the literal reasoning of bandbox and counter-hopping philosophers, consoling the unfortunate by enumerating and multiplying their faults, which are always the occasion of their misfortune and so clearly to be seen after the event has occurred. I would rather at any time take an emetic than to be compelled to listen to the advice of such predicting and freakish counsellors. If I must be told of something I already know, let it be that I have learned another lesson by experience and then give me advice for the future. I have often derived a good deal of information from a person who kept silent in the crowd, and it is well known that a certain class of individuals display the most wisdom when they say the least.

On the fourth day after our arrival a large Sioux Indian, arrayed in the costume of the whites, with a sword suspended by his side, entered the lodging where I stayed and looked round on the whites for some time without speaking a word. At length he gave me a signal to follow him, and conducted me to his lodge, which I found had been prepared for the reception of a stranger. The epishemores and robes had been arranged in the back part of the lodge. I was invited to sit by my mute conductor, who, being the proprietor, seated himself on my right. The big pipe went round with the usual ceremonies and the necessary forms of Indian etiquette being complied with, mine host commenced asking questions by signs without moving his lips, and having acquired the knowledge of conversation by signs without uttering a word. It is impossible for a person not acquainted with the customs of Indians to form a correct idea in what way a continuous conversation is held for hours between two individuals who cannot understand each other's language, but frequent practice renders it faultless and I have often seen two Americans conversing by signs by way of practice. But to return to my story. My inquisitive host gathered in the course of an hour the minute details of my defeat by the Crows, with my tedious journey to the fort, and in return gave me a brief history of his life and intercourse with the whites since he had first seen them, minutely describing the battles he had been in with the Crows, the places where they were fought and their results, particularly the rank of the killed and wounded on both sides. After an hour's dumb conversation a dish of roasted buffalo tongues was set before me, accompanied by a large cake made of dried meat and fruit pounded together, mixed with buffalo marrow. It is considered an insult by an Indian for a stranger, whether white man or Indian, to return any part of the food which is set before him to eat. If there is more than he wishes to eat at one time he must, to avoid giving offense, take the remainder with him when he leaves the lodge. It is their general custom to set the best victuals their lodge affords before a stranger to eat.

On the 22d of November a small trapping party arrived, under the direction of Mr. Thomas Biggs, who intended to remain in the vicinity of the fort until he received further orders from Mr. Fontanell. On alighting from his horse, he directed his course to our lodgings. "Well, boys," said he on entering the door, "the Crows found you, did they, and could not let you go without bestowing some of their national favors upon you?" "Yes," I observed, "and we have not mended matters much by coming to this place," and related what had passed between me and the fort superintendent. "Well," said he, after I had done, "that is too ridiculous. I thought before that Mr. ——— had a soul. But I am glad I have found you here. I will see that you get such articles as you want if they can be had at this place, and you must go with me. I shall go up about fifteen miles on the Platte and encamp. I have 200 pounds of lead and powder to shoot it, and about thirty of the company's horses, which you well know were left after more than 200 were chosen out of the band to go into the Blackfoot country, and I have not one which has not from one to three of his legs standing awry, but such as they are, you are welcome to them or anything there is in the camp, even to the half of tobacco. Nearly all of my men are French and but little company for me, and I want to see you slay the fat cows and eat." So saying, he turned and walked to the apartments of his wisdom, the overseer. Presently one of the interpreters came and told us that Mr. ——— wished us to come and get our things. "Oh," said Alien, "he has got 'things,' has he, and has found out the company is owing us money? He is afraid of getting turned out of his employment by his superior. Well, let us go and get some of his things and yet inform Mr. Fontanell of his conduct." After getting our things we went to Mr. Biggs' camp as aoon as possible. Then I felt a little more independent. The rheumatism had left me and I felt as though I had rather walk than ride a poor horse. This section of country, which was called the "Black Hills," was always celebrated for the game with which it abounded. I passed most of my time hunting black tailed deer among the hills on foot, which has always been my favorite sport. One day as myself and one of my fellow hunters were traveling through the hills, coming toward us at full speed, was an immense herd of these animals. We stopped and they passed within eighty yards of us without making a halt. We shot the charges that were in our rifles, loaded, and shot two more each before they had all passed by. As the hindmost were passing I could see the foremost passing over a ridge covered with snow more than three miles distant, apparently at the same rate they had passed us. They made a trail about thirty paces wide and went in as compact a body as they consistently could. They consisted mostly of females.

CHAPTER XX

Capt. Fontanell Arrives With Property Stolen the Month Previous—
Leave for Powder River With Supplies

On the 20th day of December, 1837, Mr. Fontanell arrived at the camp with fifteen men, bringing the furs he had collected during the hunt, for the purpose of depositing them at the fort. He informed us he had left the main party on Powder River and expressed his sorrow that he had been the cause of our misfortune. He had mistaken the day agreed upon to meet at Clark's Fork, and sent two men to the place on the 18th of November, who found the note I had left. "But," said he, "I have met with that village of Crows and recovered all your property that could be identified. I told them, when I heard the circumstances, that if they did not produce your property forthwith, their heads would pay for it within twenty-four hours. On hearing this they immediately gave up, as they repeatedly affirmed, all except the beaver skins, which they had traded to a Portugese by the name of Antonio Montaro, who had built some log cabins on Powder River for the purpose of trading with the Crows." He immediately continued: "We went to the cabins and asked Mr. Montaro what right he had to trade beaver skins from Indians with white men's names marked upon them, knowing them to be stolen or taken by force from the whites, and asked him to deliver them to me, which he refused to do. I then ordered him to give me the key to his warehouse, which he reluctantly did. I then ordered my clerk to go in and take all the beaver skins he could find with your names marked upon them, and have them carried to my camp, which was done without further ceremony." Here, then, was the sum and substance of the sorrows expressed by the Crow chief, whose feelings were so much hurt to think that we were robbed by men, or dogs, belonging to his village, yet I have no doubt if we had gone with him we would have received our things and fared better than we did by the course we pursued. However, we were like all mortals of the present day—destitute of foreknowledge.

On the 28th of January the party started for Powder River with supplies for the main camp, leaving Mr. Fontanell at the fort. The weather being cold, we were compelled to travel on foot most of the time to keep ourselves from freezing. The snow was about ten inches deep generally, but drifted very much in many places. On the 7th of February we reached the encampment, all in good health, fine spirits, and with full stomachs. Here we found the camp living on the fat of the land. The bottoms along Powder River were crowded with buffaloes, so much so that it was difficult keeping them from among the horses, which were fed upon sweet cottonwood bark, as the buffaloes had consumed everything in the shape of grass along the river.

We passed the remainder of the winter very agreeably until the 25th of March, when the winter began to break, the buffaloes to leave the stream and scatter among the hills and the trappers to prepare for the spring hunt.

CHAPTER XXI

Spring Hunt—A Trapper's Equipment—Canadian Trapper Has Encounter With Grizzly Bear Without Serious Injury

After making the usual arrangements we started on the 29th down Powder River, making short marches, as our animals were very poor. On the 3d of April we left the river and traveled across the country, which was generally comprised of rolling hills, in a northerly direction until the 18th, when we reached the Little Horn River and traveled down it to the forks. This river empties into the Big Horn about forty miles below the lower mountain. April 21st we left the forks and traveled nearly west over a broken and uneven country, about eighteen miles, and encamped on a small spring branch. After we had encamped the trappers made preparations for starting the next day to hunt beaver, as we had set but few traps since we left winter quarters, for the Crows had destroyed nearly all the beaver in the part of the country through which we had been traveling. Early next morning about thirty of us were armed, equipped and mounted, as circumstances required. A trapper's equipment in such cases is generally one animal upon which is placed one or two epishemores, a riding saddle and bridle, a sack containing six beaver traps, a blanket with an extra pair of moccasins, his powder horn and bullet pouch, with a belt to which is attached a butcher knife, a wooden box containing bait for beaver, a tobacco sack with a pipe and implements for making fire, with sometimes a hatchet fastened to the pommel of his saddle. His personal dress is a flannel or cotton shirt (if he is fortunate enough to obtain one, if not antelope skin answers the purpose of over and undershirt), a pair of leather breeches with blanket or smoked buffalo skin leggings, a coat made of blanket or buffalo robe, a hat or cap of wool, buffalo or otter skin, his hose are pieces of blanket wrapped around his feet, which are covered with a pair of moccasins made of dressed deer, elk or buffalo skins, with his long hair falling loosely over his shoulders, completes his uniform. He then mounts and places his rifle before him on his saddle. Such was the dress equipage of the party, myself included, now ready to start. After getting the necessary information from Mr. Bridger concerning the route he intended to take with the camp, we all started in a gallop in a westerly direction and traveled to the Big Horn and there commenced separating by twos and threes in different directions. I crossed the river with the largest party, still keeping a west course, most of the time in a gallop, until sun about an hour high at night, when we killed a bull and each taking some of the meat for supper proceeded on our journey till sunset, when I found myself with only one companion. All had turned to the right or left without once hinting their intentions, for it was not good policy for a trapper to let too many know where he intended to set his traps, particularly if his horse is not as fast as those of his companions. I am sure my remaining companion, who was a Canadian Frenchman, knew not where I intended to set until I stopped my horse at a beaver dam between sunset and dark. We set three traps each and went down the stream half a mile and encamped some time after dark. This day I had traveled about forty miles with a poor horse, over a rough and broken country, intersected with deep ravines. The next morning we set the remainder of our traps and started down the stream about a mile, where we found two more trappers. We encamped with them, hobbled our horses and turned them out to feed, and before night our numbers had increased to twelve men. The camp came to us on the 26th of April, and found us nearly all together. We raised our traps and moved on with them to the West Fork of Prior's River, where we arrived on the 29th. The next morning we made another start, as formerly. My intentions were to set my traps on Rocky Fork, which we reached about three o'clock PM, our party having diminished to three men beside myself. In the meanwhile it began to rain and we stopped to approach a band of buffaloes, and as myself and one of my comrades (a Canadian) were walking along, half bent, near some bushes, secreting ourselves from the buffalo, a large grizzly bear, which probably had been awakened from his slumbers by our approach, sprang upon the Canadian, who was five or six feet before me, and placing one fore paw upon his head and the other on his left shoulder, pushed him to one side about twelve feet with as little ceremony as if he had been a cat, still keeping a direct course as though nothing had happened. I called to the Canadian and soon found the fright exceeded the wound, as he had received no injury except what this impudent stranger had done by tearing his coat, but it was hard telling which was the most frightened, the man or the bear. We reached Rocky Fork about sunset and going along the edge of the timber saw another bear lying down with a buffalo calf which he had already killed between his forepaws, while the mother was standing about twenty paces distant, moaning very pitifully for the loss of her young. The bear, on seeing us, dropped the calf and took to his heels into the brush. The next day we traveled up Rocky Fork till about eleven o'clock, when I discovered there were trappers ahead of me. I then altered my course, leaving the stream at right angles in a westerly direction, and traveled across the country, parallel with the mountain, in company with a Canadian, for about ten miles, set my traps on a stream called Bodair's Fork (named after a Canadian who was killed by the Blackfeet in 1836). After setting our traps we traveled down the stream, encamped, and before night our party consisted of fifteen men who had set their traps and come to this place to spend the night without any previous arrangement whatever. But an old trapper can form some idea where his companions will encamp, though they seldom tell before their traps are set. I stopped at this place until the 6th of May, when, learning that the camp had arrived on Rocky Fork below, I left my traps and went to it to get a fresh horse. On the 7th the camp moved near to where my traps were set and the next day moved on to the right hand fork of the Rosebud. 9th—I raised my traps and overtook them at the junction of the three forks of the Rosebud. The next day I started with two more to trap the head streams of this river. We traveled up the middle fork to the mountains, where we found signs of four or five trappers before us, and to follow a fresh horse track in trapping time is neither wise nor profitable with such a number of trappers as our camp contained. On the 14th we started to the camp, which we found on the Yellowstone at the mouth of the cross creeks. The next day the camp crossed the Yellowstone and moved up the north side to the mouth of "Twenty-five Yard" River. There I stopped with the camp till the 19th, when I started again with three others. Traveled up "Twenty-five Yard" River about twenty-five miles in a northerly direction, then left it and took around a low point of mountains in a westerly direction and fell on to a branch of the same river which forms a half circle from the north point of the mountain from where we first struck the river. We found this part of the country had been recently trapped by the Blackfeet.

The next morning, May 20th, two of my comrades returned to the camp, as it rained very hard. The other asked me which way I was going. I replied, "To hunt beaver," and started off as I spoke. He mounted his horse and followed me without further ceremony. We left the stream and took up the mountain in a southwesterly direction. After traveling about six miles we fell into a defile running through the mountains on to Cherry River, a branch of the Yellowstone. We traveled down this branch until near night and encamped. The next day continued down the stream and reached the plains about three o'clock PM, within about twenty-five miles of the junction of the three forks of the Missouri. We here left the stream we had descended and took up a small right hand fork of it in an easterly direction, where we remained until the camp arrived on the 25th. 27th—We moved with the camp to the Gallatin Fork the next day. We crossed it with some difficulty but without accident, except the loss of three rifles. The current ran so swift that several horses lost their footing and were washed down the stream, which compelled their riders to abandon both horses and guns and swim ashore. May 29th—Traveled up this stream to the mountain, about fifteen miles, and encamped. This valley is the largest in the Rocky Mountains, except the valley of the Snake River, but far smoother than the latter and more fertile. May 30th—Traveled up the Gallatin Fork about ten miles into the mountains and encamped. 31st—We traveled up a small branch in a westerly direction about twenty-five miles. June 1st—We crossed the mountains in the same direction and encamped in the valley on the Madison Fork which, after leaving the valley, runs through a deep, rocky canyon into the plains below.

CHAPTER XXII

Battle with the Blackfeet in Which the Trappers Were the Aggressors and Victors

June 2d—We crossed this fork and traveled up on the west side about fifteen miles, on a trail made by a village of Blackfeet which had passed up three or four days previously. They were, to all appearances, occasionally dying of the smallpox, which had made terrible havoc among the Blackfeet during that winter. That day we passed an Indian lodge standing in the prairie near the river, which contained nine dead bodies. 3d—Continued up the stream on their trail until ten o'clock AM, when Mr. Bridger, having charge of the camp, tried to avoid them by taking into the mountains, but the majority of the men remonstrated so hard against trying to avoid a village of Blackfeet which did not contain more than three times our number, that he altered his course, and turned back toward the Madison and encamped about two miles from the river on a small spring branch. This branch ran through a ridge in a narrow passage of rocks, a hundred feet perpendicular on both sides, about a quarter of a mile from the Madison. The next morning as we were passing over the ridge around this place, we discovered the village about three miles above us on the river. We immediately drove into the canyon with the camp and prepared for battle. Our leader was no military commander, therefore no orders were given. After the company property was secured about fifteen men mounted horses and started for the village in order to commence a skirmish. The village was situated on the west bank of the river. About thirty rods behind it arose a bench of land 100 feet high, running parallel with the river and gradually ascending to the westward until it terminated in a high range of mountains about two miles distant. While our men were approaching the village I took a telescope and ascended the highest point of rocks which overhung the camp, to view the maneuvers. They rode within a short distance of the edge of the bench, then dismounted and crept to the edge and opened fire on the village, which was the first the Indians knew of our being in the country. They fired three or four rounds each before the Indians had time to mount their horses and ascend the bluff 150 yards above them. The whites then mounted their horses and returned towards the camp before about five times their number. A running fire was kept up on both sides until our men reached the camp, when the Indians took possession of an elevated point formed of broken rock, about 300 paces distant on the south side of the camp, from which they kept shooting at intervals for about two hours without doing any damage. Presently one of them called to us in the Flathead tongue and said that we were not men, but women, and had better dress ourselves as such, for we had bantered them to fight and then crept into the rocks like women. An old Iroquois trapper who had been an experienced warrior, trained on the shores of Lake Superior, understanding this harangue, turned to the whites about him and made a speech in imperfect English nearly as follows: "My friends, you see dat Ingun talk? He no talk good, he talk berry bad. He say you, me, all same like squaw. Dat no good. 'Spose you go wid me. I make him no talk dat way." On saying this he stripped himself entirely naked, throwing his powder horn and bullet pouch over his shoulder, and taking his rifle in his hand, began to dance and utter the shrill war cry of his nation. Twenty of us who stood around and near him cheered the sound which had been the death warrant of so many whites during the old French war. He started and we followed, amid a shower of balls. The distance, as I said before, was about 300 yards up a smooth and gradual ascent to the rocks where the Blackfeet had secreted themselves to the number of 150. The object of our leader was to make an open charge and drive them from their position, which we effected without loss, under an incessant storm of fusee balls. When we reached the rocks we stopped to breathe for about half a minute, not having as yet discharged a single gun. We then mounted over the piles of granite and attacked them muzzle to muzzle. Although seven or eight times our number, they retreated from rock to rock like hunted rats among the ruins of an old building, whilst we followed close at their heels, loading and shooting, until we drove them entirely into the plain where their horses were tied. They carried off their dead, with the exception of two, and threw them into the river. They placed their wounded on horses and started slowly towards their village with a mournful cry. We then packed our animals and followed them with the camp within a quarter of a mile of the village, where we stopped for the night. During the night they moved the village up about three miles further. Next morning we ascended the bench, intending to pass with the camp by the village. We soon found, however, that they had formed a line of mounted warriors from the river to the thick pines which grew on the mountain. About thirty of us concluded to try the bravery of those cavaliers on the field, leaving the remainder of the camp to bring up the rear. Under cover of the camp we rode into a thicket, out of their sight, and turned into a deep ravine, which led us, undiscovered, within twenty or thirty paces of their line. They, in the meantime, were watching the motions of the camp, intending to attack it while crossing the ravine. We approached nearly to the top of the bank, where we concluded to rest our horses a moment and then charge their line in front near the left wing. We were close enough to hear them talking as they pranced back and forth on the bench above us. After tightening our girths and examining our arms, each of us put four or five bullets in our mouths and mounted without noise. Our leader (the same old Iroquois) sallied forth with a horrid yell, and we followed. The Indians were so much surprised with such a sudden attack that they made no resistance whatever, but wheeled and took toward the village as fast as their horses could carry them, whilst we pursued close at their heels until within about 300 yards of their lodges, where we made a halt and stopped until the camp had passed, then rode quietly away to our own party. After leaving them we traveled up the Madison about eight miles and encamped near the place where we had fought the Blackfeet in September, 1835. The Madison, after leaving the mountains, runs westerly to this place, forms a curve, and, turning east of north, in which direction it runs, to the junction of the three forks. The next day, June 6th, we left the Madison and traveled south over an undulating plain, about fifteen miles, and encamped at Henry Lake. This lake is about thirty miles in circumference, surrounded by forests of pine, except on the southeast side, where there is a small prairie about one mile wide and two long, terminating almost to a point at the two extremities. Here we discovered another village of Blackfeet of about fifteen lodges, who were encamped on our route at the southeast side of the lake. The next morning we concluded to move camp to the village and smite it, without leaving one to tell their fate, but when within about two miles of the village we met six of them coming to us unarmed, who invited us in the most humble and submissive manner to their village to smoke and trade. This proceeding conquered the bravest in our camp, for we were ashamed to think of fighting a few poor Indians, nearly dwindled to skeletons by the smallpox, and approaching us without arms. We stopped, however, and traded with them and then started on our journey, encamping at night in the edge of the pine woods. June 8th—We commenced our march through the pine woods by the lower track, which runs south nearly parallel with the course of

Henry's Fork, and on the 11th we emerged from the pine woods into the plains of Snake River, where we stopped and trapped until the 14th. From thence we went to Pierre's Hole, where we found a party of ten trappers who had left the party at the mouth of "Twenty-five Yard River." They had been defeated by the Blackfeet, lost most of their horses, and one man was wounded in the thigh by a fusee ball.

CHAPTER XXIII

Routine Experiences Followed by the Regular July (1838) Rendezvous on Green River—Fall Hunt

June 18th—We left Pierre's Hole and crossed the mountain to Jackson's Big Hole. The next day myself and another trapper left the camp, crossed Lewis Fork and traveled down the valley to the south end. The next day we traveled in a southwest direction over high and rugged spurs of mountain and encamped on a small stream running into Gray's River, which empties into Lewis Fork above the mouth of Salt River. 21st—Traveled down the stream to Gray's River and set traps. We remained hunting the small streams which ran into this river until the 28th of June, then crossed the mountains in a southeast direction and fell on to a stream running into Green River, about thirty-five miles below the mouth of Horse Creek, called Seborges Fork. July 1st—We traveled down this stream to the plains and steered our course northeast towards Horse Creek, where we expected to find the rendezvous. The next day we arrived at the place, but instead of finding the camp we found a large band of buffaloes near the appointed, place of meeting. We rode up to an old log building which was formerly used as a store house during the rendezvous, where I discovered a piece of paper fastened upon the wall, which informed me that we should find the whites at the forks of Wind River. This was unwelcome news to us, as our animals were very much jaded. We then went down Green River, crossed and encamped for the night. The next day we traveled to Little Sandy. 3d—We camped on the point of the mountain on a branch of Sweetwater. 4th—We encamped at the Oil Spring on Popo-azia, and the next day we arrived at the camp. There we found Mr. Dripps from St. Louis, with twenty horse carts loaded with supplies, and again met Captain Stewart, likewise several missionaries with their families on their way to the Columbia River. On the 8th Mr. F. Ermatinger arrived with a small party from the Columbia, accompanied by the Rev. Jason Lee, who was on his way to the United States. On the 20th of July the meeting broke up and the parties again dispersed for the fall hunt.

I started, with about thirty trappers, up Wind River, expecting the camp to follow in a few days. During our stay at the rendezvous it was rumored among the men that the company intended to bring no more supplies to the Rocky Mountains, and discontinue all further operations. This caused a great deal of discontent among the trappers and numbers left the party. 21st—We traveled up Wind River about thirty miles and encamped. 22d—Continued up the river till noon, then left it to our right, traveled over a high ridge covered with pines, in a westerly direction about fifteen miles, and fell on to the Grosvent Fork. Next day we traveled about twenty miles down Grosvent Fork. 24th—Myself and another crossed the mountain in a northwest direction, fell on to a stream running into Lewis Fork, about ten miles below Jackson's Lake. Here we stayed and trapped until the 29th. Then we started back to the Grosvent Fork, where we found the camp, consisting of about sixty men, under the direction of Mr. Dripps, with James Bridger pilot.

The next day the camp followed down the Grosvent Fork to Jackson's Hole. In the meantime myself and comrade returned to our traps, which we raised, and took over the mountain in a southwest direction and overtook the camp on Lewis Fork. The whole company was starving. Fortunately I had killed a deer in crossing the mountain, which made supper for the whole camp. Aug. 1st—We crossed Lewis Fork and encamped and stayed the next day. 3d—Camp crossed the mountain to Pierre's Hole and the day following I started with my former comrade to hunt beaver on the streams which ran from the Yellowstone. About the middle of the afternoon, as we were winding down a steep declivity which overhung a precipice of rock nearly 200 feet perpendicular, my horse slipped and fell headlong down and was dashed to pieces. 6th—I returned to camp in Pierre's valley. On the next day made another start with the same comrade. After leaving camp we traveled in a southwest direction across the valley, then took over low hills, covered with pines until sun about an hour high, when we stopped and set our traps. On the 8th we traveled down the stream about three miles and then ascended a left hand branch in a northeasterly direction. After traveling about ten miles we fell into a valley surrounded by high mountains, except on the southwest side. This valley was about four miles long and one mile wide, whilst the huge piles of rock reaching above the clouds seemed almost to overhang the place on the north and east sides. We stopped here on the 9th and on the 10th returned to hunt the camp. When leaving we took up the valley in a westerly direction and from thence traveled a northwest course through dense forests of pines about fifteen miles, when we struck the trail of the camp going north. We followed the track, which still led us through the forest, about twelve miles, when we came to a prairie about five miles in circumference in which the camp had stopped the night previous. We stopped here a few minutes, then resumed our journey on the trail, and after winding about among the fallen trees and rocks about six miles, we fell on to the middle branch of Henry's Fork, which is called by hunters "The Falling Fork," from the numerous cascades it forms whilst meandering through the forest previous to its junction with the main river. At the place where we struck the fork is one of the most beautiful cascades I have ever seen. The stream is about sixty yards wide and falls over the rocks in a straight line about thirty feet perpendicular. It is very deep and still above where it breaks, and it gradually shallows to the depth of three feet on the brink. It is also very deep below and almost dead, except the motion caused by the waters falling into the deep, pond-like stream and boiling from the bottom, rolling off into small riffles and dying away into a calm, smooth surface.

We ascended this stream, passing several beautiful cascades, for about twelve miles, where the trail led us into a prairie seven or eight miles in circumference, in which we found the camp just as the sun was setting.

The next morning, August 11th, we bid adieu to the camp and started on the back track to trap the stream we had left the day previous. However, we took a nearer route and reached the little valley, where we stayed until the 25th. This day we had a tremendous thunder storm, which broke in peals against the towering rocks above us with such dreadful clashing that it seemed as if they would have been torn from their foundations and hurled into the valley upon our heads. Such storms are very frequent about these mountains and often pass over without rain.

27th—We left the valley and ascended the mountain southwest and traveled about fifteen miles to a branch of Henry's Fork. Here we stayed until the 7th of September, and then started down Henry's Fork southwest. After traveling about twelve miles we left the pines and traveled parallel with the stream over rolling ridges among scattered groves of quaking asps, when we arrived at the edge of the plains in traveling about eight miles. Here we discovered a trail made by a war party of Blackfeet, evidently the night previous. we then took a course south and traveled our horses in a trot all day and encamped an hour after dark on Lewis Fork, about fifteen miles above the junction. The next day we traveled to Blackfoot Creek and the day following to Fort Hall. We remained at the fort until the 20th, and then started down Snake River trapping, with a party of ten men beside ourselves.

CHAPTER XXIV

Returned to Fort Hall and Remained in That Vicinity Till January of 1839—Spring Hunt

22d—We arrived at a stream called Cozzu (or Raft River). This we ascended and hunted until the 5th of October, when, finding the country had been recently hunted, we returned to Fort Hall. From thence we started on the 18th with the fort hunter and six men to kill and dry buffalo meat for the winter. We cruised about on the Snake River and its waters until the 23d of November, when the weather becoming very cold, and snow about fifteen inches deep, we returned with our horses loaded with meat to Fort Hall. We stopped here until the 1st of January, 1839, when we began to be tired of dried meat, and concluded to move up the river to where Lewis Fork leaves the mountain and there spend the remainder of the winter, killing and eating mountain sheep.

There were six in the company and we started on the 2d traveling slowly, as the snow was deep and the weather cold, and arrived at the destined place on the 20th of January. We were followed by seven lodges of Snake Indians. We found the snow shallow about the foot of the mountain, with plenty of sheep, elk, and some few bulls among the rocks and low spurs.

26th—I, with two white men and several Indians, started through the canyon to hunt elk. After traveling about four miles, I left the party and took up the river on the north side, whilst the remainder crossed the river on the ice to follow the trail of some bulls. I ascended the river, traveling on the ice and land alternately, about four miles further and encamped for the night. This was a severe, cold night, but I was comfortably situated with one blanket and two epishemores and plenty of dry wood to make a fire. When I arose in the morning I discovered a band of elk about half a mile up the mountain. I took my tifle and went to approach them through the snow three feet deep, and when within about 250 paces of them they took the wind of me and ran off, leaving me to return to my encampment with the consolation that this was not the first time the wind had blown away my breakfast. When I arrived at my camp, I found plenty of fresh buffalo meat hanging on the bushes near where I had slept. I immediately began to roast and eat, as twenty-four hours' fasting would naturally dictate. Presently a Snake Indian arrived to whom the meat belonged.

Near where I was encamped was a small stream which ran from a spring about 100 paces distant and emptied into the river. The water was a little more than blood warm. The beaver had taken advantage of the situation, dammed it up at the mouth and built a large lodge on the bank. At sunrise I discovered three of them swimming and playing in the water.

The next day I killed a bull and returned, through the canyon, to our camp.

On the 30th I started, with my old comrade (Elbridge), back with our traps to try the beaver. The snow was about two feet deep on the level plain and it took us till near night to reach the place. We encamped in a cave at the foot of the mountain near by and I set four traps. The weather was extremely cold, but I felt very comfortable while walking around in the warm water. On coming out and running as fast as I could to the camp, forty rods distant, both my feet were frozen. I soon drew out the frost, however, by stripping them and holding them in the cold snow. Next morning I found four large, fat beavers in my traps, and on the 2d day of February we returned to camp with twelve beavers.

February 10th—Moved with the camp up the river to where we had caught the beaver and encamped. Lewis's Fork comes through this canyon for about twelve miles, where the rock rises 200 or 300 feet, forms a bench and ascends gradually to the mountain, which approaches very close on the north side, and on the south side is about three or four miles distant. An occasional ravine running from the mountain to the river through the rocks on the north side forms convenient places for camping, as the bench and low spurs are well clothed with bunch grass. Here we found immense numbers of mountain sheep, which the deep snows had driven down to the low points of rock facing the south near the river. We could see them nearly every morning from our lodges, standing on the points of rock jutting out so high in the air that they appeared no larger than weasels. It is in this position that a hunter delights to approach them from behind and shoot, whilst their eyes are fixed on some object below. It is an exercise which gives vigor, health, and appetite to the hunter, to shoulder his rifle at daybreak on a clear, cold morning and wind his way up a rugged mountain, over rocks and crags, at length killing a fat old ewe and taking the meat to camp on his back. This kind of exercise gives him an appetite for his breakfast. But hunting sheep is attended with great danger in many places, especially when the rocks are covered with sleet and ice. I have often passed over places where I have had to cut steps in the ice with my butcher knife in which to place my feet, directly over the most frightful precipices, but being excited in the pursuit of game, I would think but little of danger until I had laid down to sleep at night. Then it would make my blood run cold to meditate upon the scenes I had passed through during the day, and often have I resolved never to risk myself in such places again and as often broken the resolution. The sight of danger is less hideous than the thought of it.

On the 18th of March the winter commenced breaking up with a heavy rain, and four of us started up the river to commence the spring hunt, whilst the remainder of the party returned to the fort. After traveling through the canyon we found the ground bare in many places, whilst it still continued to rain. On the 30th of March we traveled to the mouth of Muddy. This we ascended and crossed the mountain with some difficulty, as the snow was very deep, on to the head waters of Gray's Creek. There two of our party (who were Canadians) left us and struck off for themselves. Our camp then consisted of myself and my old comrade, Elbridge. I say old comrade because we had been some time together, but he was a young man, from Beverly, Mass., and being bred a sailor, he was not much of a landsman, woodsman or hunter, but a great, easy, good-natured fellow, standing five feet ten inches and weighing 200 pounds.

On the 20th of April we crossed a high ridge in a north direction and encamped on a stream that sinks in the plain soon after leaving the mountain. Here we set our traps for beaver, but their dams were nearly all covered with ice, excepting some few holes which they had made for the purpose of obtaining fresh provisions. We stopped on this stream until the 26th of April and then traveled out by the same way which we came.

26th—We traveled in a southerly direction about twenty-five miles, crossing several of the head branches of Gray's Creek. On the 1st of May we traveled about ten miles east course and the next day went to the head of Gray's marsh, about twenty miles south course. There we deposited the furs we had taken, and the next day started for Salt River to get a supply of salt. We took an easterly direction about six miles and fell on to Gardner's Fork, which we descended to the valley, and on the 6th arrived at the Salt Springs on Scott's Fork of Salt River. Here we found twelve of our old comrades who had come, like ourselves, to gather salt. We stayed two nights together at this place, when Elbridge and myself took leave of them and returned to Gray's marsh. From there we started toward Fort Hall, traveling one day and laying by five or six to fatten our horses, and arrived at the fort on the 5th of June.

CHAPTER XXV

Another Viewpomt of What Is Now Known as the Yellowstone National Park

This fort now belonged to the British Hudson Bay Company, who obtained it by purchase from Mr. Wyeth in the year 1837. We stopped at the fort until the 26th of June, then made up a party of four for the purpose of trapping in the Yellowstone and Wind Mountains, and arrived at Salt River valley on the 28th. 29th—We crossed the valley northeast, then left it, ascending Gray's River in an easterly direction about four miles, into a narrow, rugged pass, encamped and killed a sheep. 30th—We traveled up this stream thirty miles east and encamped in a small valley and killed a bull, and the next day we encamped in the south end of Jackson's Hale. July 2d—We traveled through the valley north until night, and the next day arrived at Jackson's Lake, where we concluded to spend the Fourth of July at the outlet.

July 4th—I caught about twenty very fine silver trout, which, together with fat mutton, buffalo beef, and coffee, and the manner in which it was ground up, constituted a dinner that ought to be considered independent, even by Britons.

July 5th—We traveled north parallel with the lake, on the east side, and the next day arrived at the inlet or northern extremity. 7th—We left the lake and followed up Lewis's Fork about eight miles in a northeasterly direction and encamped. On the day following we traveled about five miles, when we came to the junction of two equal forks. We took up the left hand on the west side, through the thick pines, and in many places so much fallen timber that we frequently had to make circles of a quarter of a mile to gain a few rods ahead, but our general course was north, and I suppose we traveled about sixteen miles in that direction. At night we encamped at a lake about fifteen miles in circumference, which formed the stream we had ascended. July 9th—We traveled round this lake to the inlet on the west side, and came to another lake about the same size. This had a small prairie on the west side, whilst the other was completely surrounded by thick pines. The next day we traveled along the border of the lake till we came to the northwest extremity, where we found about fifty springs of boiling hot water. We stopped here some hours, as one of my comrades had visited this spot the year previous and wished to show us some curiosities. The first spring we visited was about ten feet in diameter, which threw up mud with a noise similar to boiling soap. Close about this were numerous springs similar to it, throwing up mud and water five or six feet high. About thirty or forty paces from these, along the side of a small ridge, the hot steam rushed forth from holes in the ground, with a hissing noise which could be heard a mile distant. On a near approach we could hear the water bubbling underground, some distance from the surface.

The sound of our footsteps over this place was like thumping over a hollow vessel of immense size. In many places were peaks from two to six feet high formed of limestone, which appeared of a snowy whiteness, deposited by the boiling water. The water, when cold, was perfectly sweet, except having a fresh limestone taste. After surveying these natural wonders for some time my comrade conducted me to what he called the "Hour Spring." At that spring the first thing which attracted the attention was a hole about fifteen inches in diameter in which the water was boiling slowly about four inches below the surface. At length it began to boil and bubble violently and the water commenced raising and shooting upwards until the column arose to the height of sixty feet, from whence it fell to the ground in drops in a circle about thirty feet in diameter, perfectly cold when it struck the ground. It continued shooting up in this manner five or six minutes and then sank back to its former state of slowly boiling for an hour and then it would shoot forth again as before. My comrade said he had watched the motions of this spring for one whole day and part of the night the year previous and found no irregularity whatever in its movements. After surveying these wonders for a few hours we left the place and traveled north about three miles over ascending ground, then descended a steep and rugged mountain four miles in the same direction and fell on to the head branch of the Jefferson branch of the Missouri. The whole country was still thickly covered with pines except here and there a small prairie. We encamped and set some traps for beaver and stayed four days. At this place there was also a large number of hot springs, some of which had formed cones of limestone twenty feet high of a snowy whiteness, which makes a splendid appearance standing among the evergreen pines. Some of the lower peaks are very convenient for the hunter in preparing his dinner when hungry, for here his kettle is always ready and boiling. His meat being suspended in the water by a string is soon prepared for his meal without further trouble. Some of these spiral cones are twenty feet in diameter at the base and not more than twelve inches at the top, the whole being covered with small, irregular semicircular ridges about the size of a man's finger, having the appearance of carving in bas relief, formed, I suppose, by the waters running over it for ages unknown. I should think this place to be 3,000 feet lower than the springs we left on the mountain. Vast numbers of black tailed deer are found in the vicinity of these springs and seem to be very familiar with hot water and steam, the noise of which seems not to disturb their slumbers, for a buck may be found carelessly sleeping where the noise will exceed that of three or four engines in operation. Standing upon an eminence and superficially viewing these natural monuments, one is half inclined to believe himself in the neighborhood of the ruins of some ancient city, whose temples had been constructed of the whitest marble.

July 15th—We traveled down the stream northwest about 12 miles, passing on our route large numbers of hot springs with their snow white monuments scattered among the groves of pines. At length we came to a boiling lake about 300 feet in diameter, forming nearly a complete circle as we approached on the south side. The steam which arose from it was of three distinct colors. From the west side for one-third of the diameter it was white, in the middle it was pale red, and the remaining third on the east, light sky blue. Whether it was something peculiar in the state of the atmosphere, the day being cloudy, or whether it was some chemical properties contained in the water which produced this phenomenon, I am unable to say, and shall leave the explanation to some scientific tourist who may have the curiosity to visit this place at some future period. The water was of deep indigo blue, boiling like an immense cauldron, running over the white rock which had formed around the edges to the height of four or five feet from the surface of the earth, sloping gradually for sixty or seventy feet. What a field of speculation this presented for chemist and geologist.

The next morning we crossed the stream, traveled down the east side about five miles, then ascended another fork in an easterly direction about ten miles and encamped. From where we left the main fork it runs in a northwest direction about forty miles before reaching the Burnt Hole. July 17th—We traveled to the head of this branch, about twenty miles, east direction. 18th—After traveling in the same direction about seven miles over a low spur of the mountains, we came into a large plain on the Yellowstone River, about eight miles below the lake, and followed up the Yellowstone to the outlet of the lake and encamped and set our traps for beaver. We stopped here trapping until the 28th and from thence we traveled to the "Secluded Valley," where we stayed one day. From there we traveled east to the head of Clark's Fork, where we stopped and hunted the small branches until the 4th of August, and then returned to the valley. On the 9th we left the valley and traveled two days over the mountains northwest and fell on to a stream running south into the Yellowstone, where we stayed until the 16th, and then crossed the mountain, in a northwest direction, over the snow, and fell on to a stream running into the Yellowstone plains and entering that river about forty miles above the mouth of "Twenty-five Yard River." 18th—We descended this stream within about a mile of the plain and set our traps.

The next day my comrades started for the plains to kill some buffalo cows. I remonstrated very hard against them going into the plains and disturbing the buffaloes in such a dangerous part of the country, when we had plenty of fat deer and mutton, but to no purpose. Off they started and returned at night with their animals loaded with cow meat. They told me they had seen where a village of 300 or 400 lodges of Blackfeet had left the Yellowstone in a northwesterly direction but three or four days previous. Aug. 22d—We left this stream and traveled along the foot of the mountains at the edge of the plain, about twenty miles west course, and encamped at a spring. The next day we crossed the Yellowstone River and traveled up the river on the west side to the mouth of Gardner's Fork, where we stayed the next day. 25th—We traveled to "Gardner's Hole," then altered our course southeast, crossing the eastern point of the valley, and encamped on a small branch among the pines. 26th—We encamped on the Yellowstone in the big plain below the lake. The next day we went to the lake and set our traps on a branch running into it, near the outlet on the northeast side.

CHAPTER XXVI

Wounded by Arrows of Blackfeet—Hair-Raising Experience—
Hospitable Reception at Fort Hall

28th—After visiting my traps I returned to the camp, where, after stopping about an hour or two, I took my rifle and sauntered down the shore of the lake among the scattered groves of tall pines until tired of walking about (the day being very warm), I took a bath in the lake, probably half an hour, and returned to the camp about four o'clock PM. Two of my comrades observed, "Let us take a walk among the pines and kill an elk," and started off, whilst the other was lying asleep. Some time after they were gone I went to a bale of dried meat which had been spread in the sun thirty or forty feet from the place where we slept. Here I pulled off my powder horn and bullet pouch, laid them on a log, drew my butcher knife and began to cut. We were encamped about a half mile from the lake on a stream running into it in a southwest direction through a prairie bottom about a quarter of a mile wide. On each side of this valley arose a bench of land about twenty feet high, running parallel with the stream and covered with pines. On this bench we were encamped on the southeast side of the stream. The pines immediately behind us were thickly intermingled with logs and fallen trees. After eating a few minutes I arose and kindled a fire, filled my tobacco pipe and sat down to smoke. My comrade, whose name was White, was still sleeping. Presently I east my eyes toward the horses, which were feeding in the valley, and discovered the heads of some Indians who were gliding round under the bench within thirty steps of me. I jumped to my rifle and aroused White. Looking towards my powder horn and bullet pouch, it was already in the hands of an Indian, and we were completely surrounded. We cocked our rifles and started through their ranks into the woods, which seemed to be completely filled with Blackfeet, who rent the air with their horrid yells. On presenting our rifles, they opened a space about twenty feet wide, through which we plunged. About the fourth jump an arrow struck White on the right hip joint. I hastily told him to pull it out and as I spoke another arrow struck me in the same place, but this did not retard our progress. At length another arrow struck through my right leg beneath the flesh and above the knee, so that I fell with my breast across a log. The Indian who shot me was within eight feet of me and made a spring toward me with his uplifted battle ax. I made a leap and dodged the blow and kept hopping from log to log through a shower of arrows which flew around us like hail, lodging in the pines and logs. After we had passed them about ten paces we wheeled and took aim at them. They began to dodge behind the trees and shoot their guns. We then ran and hopped about fifty yards further in the lops and bushes and made a stand. I was very faint from the loss of blood and we sat down among the logs, determined to kill the two foremost when they came up and then die like men. We rested our rifles across a log, White aiming at the foremost and myself at the second. I whispered to him that when they turned their eyes toward us to pull trigger. About twenty of them passed by us within fifteen feet without casting a glance toward us. Another file came round on the opposite side within twenty or thirty paces, closing with the first few a few rods beyond us and all turning to the right, the next minute were out of sight among the bushes. They were well armed with fusees, bows, and battle axes. We sat until the rustling among the bushes had died away, then arose, and after looking carefully around us, White asked in a whisper how far it was to the lake. I replied, pointing to the southeast, about a quarter of a mile. I was nearly fainting from the loss of blood and the want of water. We hobbled along forty or fifty rods and I was obliged to sit down a few minutes, then go a little further and rest again. We managed in this way until we reached the bank of the lake. Our next object was to obtain some of the water, as the bank was very steep and high. White had been perfectly calm and delibe-rate until now. His conversation became wild, hurried and despairing. He observed, "I cannot go down to that water, for I am wounded all over. I shall die." I told him to sit down while I crawled down and brought some in my hat. This I effected with a great deal of difficulty. We then hobbled along the border of the lake for a mile and a half, when it grew dark and we stopped. We could still hear the shouting of the savages over their booty. We stopped under a lame pine tree near the lake, and I told White I could go no further.

"Oh," said he, "let us go into the pines and find a spring." I replied there was no spring within a mile of us, which I knew to be a fact. "Well," said he, "if you stop here I shall make a fire." "Make as much as you please," I replied angrily. "This is a poor time now to undertake to frighten me." I then started to the water, crawling on my hands and one knee, and returned in about an hour with some in my hat. While I was at this he had kindled a small fire, and taking a draught of water from the hat he exclaimed, "Oh, dear, we shall die here; we shall never get out of these mountains." "Well," said I, "if you persist in thinking so you will die, but I can crawl from this place on my hands and one knee and kill two or three elk and make a shelter of the skins, dry the meat, until we get able to travel." In this manner I persuaded him that we were not in half so bad a situation as we might be, although he was not in half so bad a situation as I expected, for, on examining I found only a slight wound from an arrow on his hip bone. But he was not so much to blame, as he was a young man who had been brought up in Missouri, the pet of the family, and had never done or learned much of anything but horse racing and gambling whilst under the care of his parents (if care it could be called). I pulled off an old piece of a coat made of blanket (as he was entirely without clothing except his hat and shirt), set myself in a leaning position against a tree, ever and anon gathering such branches and rubbish as I could reach without altering the position of my body, to keep up a little fire, and in this manner miserably spent the night. The next morning, August 29, I could not arise without assistance, when White procured a couple of sticks for crutches, by the help of which I hobbled to a small grove of pines about sixty yards distant. We had scarcely entered the grove when we heard a dog barking and Indians singing and talking. The sound seemed to be approaching us. They at length came near to where we were, to the number of sixty. Then they commenced shooting at a large band of elk that was swimming in the lake, killed four of them, dragged them to the shore and butchered them, which occupied about three hours. They then packed the meat in small bundles on their backs and traveled up along the rocky shore about a mile and encamped. We then left our hiding place and crept into the thick pines about fifty yards distant and started in the direction of our encampment in the hope of finding our comrades. My leg was very much swollen and painful, but I managed to get along slowly on my crutches by White carrying my rifle. When we were within about sixty rods of the encampment we discovered the Canadian hunting around among the trees as though he was looking for a trail. We approached him within thirty feet before he saw us, and he was so much agitated by fear that he knew not whether to run or stand still. On being asked where Elbridge was, he said they came to the camp the night before at sunset. The Indians pursued them into the woods, where they separated, and he saw him no more.

At the encampment I found a sack of salt. Everything else the Indians had carried away or cut to pieces. They had built seven large conical forts near the spot, from which we supposed their numbers to have been seventy or eighty, part of whom had returned to their village with the horses and plunder. We left the place, heaping curses on the head of the Blackfoot nation, which neither injured them nor alleviated our distress.

We followed down the shores of the lake and stopped for the night. My companions threw some logs and rubbish together, farming a kind of shelter from the night breeze, but in the night it took fire (the logs being of pitch pine) and the blaze ran to the tops of the trees. We removed a short distance, built another fire and laid by it until morning. We then made a raft of dry poles and crossed the outlet upon it. We then went to a small grove of pines nearby and made a fire, where we stopped the remainder of the day in hopes that Elbridge would see our signals and come to us, for we left directions on a tree at the encampment which route we would take. In the meantime the Canadian went to hunt something to eat, but without success. I had bathed my wounds in salt water and made a salve of beaver's oil and castorium, which I applied to them. This had eased the pain and drawn out the swelling in a great measure. The next morning I felt very stiff and sore, but we were obliged to travel or starve, as we had eaten nothing since our defeat and game was very scarce on the west side of the lake. Moreover the Canadian had got such a fright we could not prevail on him to go out of our sight to hunt. So on we trudged slowly, and after getting warm I could bear half my weight on my lame leg, but it was bent considerably and swelled so much that my knee joint was stiff. About ten o'clock the Canadian killed a couple of small ducks, which served us for breakfast. After eating them we pursued our journey. At twelve o'clock it began to rain, but we still kept on until the sun was two hours high in the evening, when the weather clearing away, we encamped at some hot springs and killed a couple of geese. Whilst we were eating them a deer came swimming along in the lake within about 100 yards of the shore. We fired several shots at him, but the water glancing the balls, he remained unhurt and apparently unalarmed, but still kept swimming to and fro in the lake in front of us for an hour and then started alone up close to the shore. The hunter went to watch it in order to kill it when it should come ashore, but as he was lying in wait for the deer a doe elk came to the water to drink and he killed her, the deer being still out in the lake swimming to and fro until dark.

Now we had plenty to eat and drink but were almost destitute of clothing. I had on a pair of trousers and a cotton shirt which were completely drenched with the rain. We made a sort of shelter from the wind out of pine branches and built a large fire of pitch knots in front of it, so that we were burning on one side and freezing on the other, alternatively, all night. The next morning we cut some of the elk meat in thin dices and cooked it slowly over a fire, then packed it in bundles, strung them on our backs and started. By this time I could carry my own rifle and limp along half as fast as a man could walk, but when my foot touched against the logs or brush the pain in my leg was very severe. We left the lake at the hot springs and traveled through the thick pines, over a low ridge of land, through the snow and rain together, but we traveled by the wind about eight miles in a southwest direction, when we came to a lake about twelve miles in circumference, which is the head spring of the right branch of Lewis's Fork. Here we found a dry spot near a number of hot springs, under some thick pines. Our hunter had killed a deer on the way and I took the skin, wrapped it around me and felt prouder of my mantle than a monarch with his imperial robes. This night I slept more than four hours, which was more than I had slept at any one time since I was wounded, and arose the next morning much refreshed. These springs were similar to those on the Madison, and among these, as well as those, sulphur was found in its purity in large quantities on the surface of the ground. We traveled along the shore on the south side about five miles in an easterly direction, fell in with a large band of elk, killed two fat does and took some of the meat. We then left the lake and traveled due south over a rough, broken country, covered with thick pines, for about twelve miles, when we came to the fork again, which ran through a narrow prairie bottom, followed down it about six miles and encamped at the forks. We had passed up the left hand fork on the 9th of July on horseback, in good health and spirits, and down on the right bank on the 31st of August on foot, with weary limbs and sorrowful countenances. We built a fire and laid down to rest, but I could not sleep more than fifteen or twenty minutes at a time, the night being so very cold. We had plenty of meat, however, and made moccasins of raw elk hide. The next day we crossed the stream and traveled down near to Jackson's Lake on the west side, then took up a small branch in a west direction to the head. We then had the Teton mountain to cross, which looked like a laborious undertaking, as it was steep and the top covered with snow. We arrived at the summit, however, with a great deal of difficulty, before sunset, and after resting a few moments, traveled down about a mile on the other side and stopped for the night. After spending another cold and tedious night, we were descending the mountain through the pines at daylight and the next night we reached the forks of Henry's Fork of Snake River. This day was very warm, but the wind blew cold at night. We made a fire and gathered some dry grass to sleep on and then sat down and ate the remainder of our provisions. It was now ninety miles to Fort Hall and we expected to see little or no game on the route, but we determined to travel it in three days. We lay down and shivered with the cold till daylight, then arose and again pursued our journey toward the fork of Snake River, where we arrived sun about an hour high, forded the river, which was nearly swimming, and encamped. The weather being very cold and fording the river so late at night, caused me much suffering during the night. Sept. 4th—We were on our way at daybreak and traveled all day through the high sage and sand down Snake River. We stopped at dark, nearly worn out with fatigue, hunger and want of sleep, as we had now traveled sixty-five miles in two days without eating. We sat and hovered over a small fire until another day appeared, then set out as usual and traveled to within about ten miles of the fort, when I was seized with a cramp in my wounded leg, which compelled me to stop and sit down every thirty or forty rods. At length we discovered a halfbreed encamped in the valley, who furnished us with horses and went with us to the fort, where we arrived about sun an hour high, being naked, hungry, wounded, sleepy, and fatigued. Here again I entered a trading post after being defeated by the Indians, but the treatment was quite different from that which I had received at Savonery's Fork in 1837, when I had been defeated by the Crows.

The fort was in charge of Mr. Courtney M. Walker, who had been lately employed by the Hudson Bay Company for that purpose. He invited us into a room and ordered supper to be prepared immediately. Likewise such articles of clothing and blankets as we called for. After dressing ourselves and giving a brief history of our defeat and sufferings, supper was brought in, consisting of tea, cakes, buttermilk, dried meat, etc. I ate very sparingly, as I had been three days fasting, but drank so much strong tea that it kept me awake till after midnight. I continued to bathe my leg in warm salt water and applied a salve, which healed it in a very short time, so that in ten days I was again setting traps for beaver. On the 13th of September Elbridge arrived safe at the fort. He had wandered about among the mountains several days without having any correct knowledge, but at length accidentally falling on to the trail which we had made in the summer, it enabled him to reach the plains and from there he traveled to the fort by his own knowledge.

On the 20th of October we started to hunt buffalo and make meat for the winter. The party consisted of fifteen men. We traveled to the head of the Jefferson Fork of the Missouri, where we killed and dried our meat. From there we proceeded over the mountains through Camas prairie to the forks of the Snake River, where most of the party concluded to spend the winter. Four of us, however, who were the only Americans in the party, returned to Fort Hall on the 10th of December. We encamped near the fort and turned our horses among the springs and timber to hunt their living during the winter, whilst ourselves were snugly arranged in our skin lodge, which was pitched among the large cottonwood trees, and in it provisions to serve us till the month of April. There were four of us in the mess. One was from Missouri, one from Massachusetts, one from Vermont, and myself from Maine. We passed an agreeable winter. We had nothing to do but to eat, attend to the horses and procure firewood. We had some few books to read, such as Byron, Shakespeare, and Scott's works, the Bible and Clark's Commentary on it, and other small works on geology, chemistry, and philosophy. The winter was very mild and the ground was bare in the valley until the 15th of January, when the snow fell about eight inches deep, but disappeared again in a few days. This was the deepest snow and of the longest duration of any we had during the winter.

CHAPTER XXVII

Old Partners "Split Blankets"—Supply Train Reaches Fort Hall on June 14, 1840

On the 10th of March I started again with my old companion Elbridge. We traveled from the fort on the Blackfoot near the foot of the mountain, where we set some traps for beaver, the ice being broken up. On the 15th we tried to cross the mountain to Gray's valley, but were compelled to turn back for the snow. On the 20th made another trial and succeeded and encamped at the forks of Gray's Creek. Here the ground was bare along the stream and on the south sides of the hills, but very deep on the high plains. I killed two bulls, which came in good time, after living on dried meat all winter. March 19th—We traveled up Gray's Creek about ten miles. There we found the snow very deep and hard enough to bear our horses in the morning. On the 22d we traveled on the snow up this stream about five miles and encamped on a bare spot of ground, where we stayed three days, then started on the snow, as usual, and went about eight miles to the valley about Gray's marsh, where we found a bare spot about forty rods square on the south side of a ridge, and encamped. The snow in the valley was about three feet deep on a level. March 28th we started on foot in the morning on the snow to hunt buffalo. After going about two miles we found eleven bulls, approached, and killed ten of them on the spot. We then butchered some of them and took out the tongues of the others, buried the meat about three feet deep in a snow drift, laid some stones on the snow over it and burned gun powder upon them to keep away the wolves. We then took meat enough for our suppers and started for the camp. By this time the snow was thawed so much that we broke through nearly every step. Early next morning, the snow being frozen, we took two horses and went for our meat, but when we reached the place where we had buried it we found the wolves had dug it up and taken the best of it, notwithstanding our precautions. The carcasses of the bulls yet remained untouched by them, and from these we loaded our horses and returned to camp. About noon the rays of the sun shining upon the snow and reflecting upward began to affect our eyes, insomuch that toward night we could scarcely look abroad. We lay down to sleep, but it was useless, for our eyes felt as if they were filled with coarse sand. After four days of severe suffering with what the trappers call snow blindness, we began to recover our eyesight by degrees, although we had not been at any time totally blind, yet we had been the whole time very near it. We stayed here until the 10th of April when, finding the snow did not abate, we returned to the forks of Gray's Creek, where we remained until the 20th. We then traveled to the fork which sinks in the plain, on Lewis's Fork, where we set our traps and stayed until the 1st of May. On the 2d we arrived again at the marsh on Gray's Creek, where we found the ground mostly bare but the streams overflowing their banks. On the 5th we crossed the mountain in an easterly direction, fell on to a stream running into Lewis's Fork ten miles below the mouth of Salt River. We traveled down this stream, which runs through a narrow cut in the mountains for about fifteen miles and then forms a small valley, where we stopped and set our traps and stayed until the 20th, when Elbridge observed he thought we had better leave our traps setting, turn and go to Salt River valley, spend a few days killing buffalo, and then return. I remonstrated against the proposal, as our horses were very poor, the streams high and the ground very muddy, but I told him if he wished to go to take his traps with him and not be at the trouble of coming back after them. The next morning he packed his horses and left me. My two horses were now my only companions, with the exception of some books which I had brought from the fort. I stayed here trapping until the 28th. Then traveled up a branch about fifteen miles, crossed the mountain in a northwest direction, fell on to the head of muddy creek, where I killed a bull and stopped for the night. The next day I stopped at this place and dried some meat. 30th—Went on the right fork of Muddy and set some traps. Here I stayed six days and then went to Gray's marsh, intending to kill and dry some meat and go to the fort, but finding no buffalo here, I crossed on to Salt River, and finding no buffalo there I ascended Gardner's Fork, crossed the mountain and fell on to Blackfoot Creek, where I killed a fat bull, dried the meat and started for Fort Hall, where I arrived on the 10th of June.

June 14th Mr. Ermatinger arrived at the fort with eighty horse loads of goods to supply the post the ensuing year. On the 15th Elbridge arrived, having fallen in with a party of hunters soon after leaving me in the mountains, after having lost his traps in crossing Gray's River. A few days after he arrived he expressed a wish that I would go with him and two others to make a hunt in the Yellowstone mountains. I replied I had seen enough of the Yellowstone mountains, and, moreover, I intended to trap in the future with a party who would not leave me in a pinch.

On the 22d of June I started with two horses, six traps, and some few books, intending to hunt on the waters of Snake River in the vicinity of Fort Hall. I went to Gray's Hole, set my traps and stayed five days. From there I went on to Milk Fork, where I stayed until the 15th of July. From there I took a northerly direction through the mountains and fell on to a stream running into Lewis Fork near the mouth of Salt River, where I stayed twelve days and then returned to Gray's marsh and stayed until the 3d of August. I then traveled through the mountains, southeast, on to the head stream of Gardner's Fork, where I spent the time hunting the small branches until the 15th. From there I started toward the fort, hunting the streams which were on the route, and arrived on the 22d.

After stopping here a few days I started, in company with three trappers, one of whom was Major Meek, and traveled to the forks of Snake River. From there we ascended

Henry's Fork about fifteen miles and then took up a stream
in a southwest direction into the mountains, but finding no
beaver, we crossed the mountain and struck Lewis's Fork in
the canyon, where, after trapping same days, we went on to
Gray's Creek, where, after staying seven days, we killed a fat
grizzly bear and some antelope, loaded the meat on our horses and started to the fort, where we arrived on the 22d of
September.

CHAPTER XXVIII

A Winter with the Indians Near Great Salt Lake—Christmas
Dinner a l' Indian

On the 1st of October I again left the fort with a Frenchman who had an Indian wife and two children, and was going on to Green River to pass the winter with them. We traveled up Portneuf about fifteen miles, where we stopped the next day and hunted antelope, and the day following we traveled up the stream about twenty miles, when, after staying ten days, we went to the Soda Springs on Bear River. Here we concluded to spend a month on Bear River, traveling slowly, hunting beaver and antelope, as the latter is the only game in this part of the country. Beaver also were getting very scarce. On the 15th of November the snow began to fall and my comrade started, with his family, across the mountains to Green River and I returned towards the fort. On my way down Bear River I met thousands of antelope traveling towards their winter quarters, which is generally Green River valley. I followed Bear River down to Cache valley, where I found twenty lodges of Snake Indians and stayed with them several days. They had a considerable number of beaver skins, but I had nothing to trade for them. They told me if I would go to the fort and get some goods, return and spend the winter with them, they would trade their furs with me. I started for the fort with one of them whom I engaged to assist me with my horses. I arrived at the fort on the 23rd of November, when, after getting such articles for trade as I wished, and my personal supplies for the winter, I returned to Cache valley, accompanied by a halfbreed. On arriving at the village I found several Frenchmen and halfbreed trappers encamped with the Snakes. One Frenchman, having an Indian wife and child, invited me to pass the winter in his lodge, and as he had a small family and large lodge, I accepted the invitation and had my baggage taken into his lodge and neatly arranged by his wife, who was a Flathead. The neat manner in which her lodge and furniture was kept would have done honor to a large portion of the "pale faced" fair sex in the civilized world.

We stayed in this valley until the 15th of December, when it was unanimously agreed to go to the Salt Lake and there spend the remainder of the winter. The next day we traveled across the valley in a southwest direction, then took into a narrow defile which led us through the mountain into the valley on the eastern borders of the lake. The day following we moved along the valley in a southerly direction and encamped on a small branch close to the foot of the mountain. The ground was still bare and the autumnal growth of grass was the best I ever saw at this season of the year.

18th—I arose about an hour before daylight, took my rifle and ascended the mountain on foot to hunt sheep. The weather was clear and cold but the mountain being steep and rugged and my rifle heavy, the exercise soon put me in a perspiration. After climbing about half a mile I sat down on a rock to wait for daylight, and when it came I discovered a band of about 100 rams within about eighty yards of me. I shot and killed one. The others ran about fifty yards further and stopped. While I was reloading my rifle one of them ascended a high pinnacle of rock which jutted over a precipice. There were others nearer me, but I wished to fetch this proud animal from his elevated position. I brought my rifle to my face, the ball whistled through his heart, and he fell headlong over the precipice. I followed the band at some distance among the crags and killed two more, butchered them, then returned and butchered the two I had first killed, and returned to camp and sent some men with horses to get the meat.

Dec. 20th—We moved along the borders of the lake about ten miles and encamped on a considerable stream running into it called Weaver's River. At this place the valley is about ten miles wide, intersected with numerous springs of salt and fresh hot and cold water, which rise at the foot of the mountain and run through the valley into the river and lake. Weaver's River is well timbered along its banks, principally with cottonwood and box elder. There are also large groves of sugar maple, pine, and some oak growing in the ravines about the mountains. We also found large numbers of elk which had left the mountains to winter among the thickets of wood and brush along the river.

Christmas

December 25th—It was agreed on by the party to prepare a Christmas dinner, but I shall first endeavor to describe the party and then the dinner. I have already said the man who was the proprietor of the lodge in which I stayed was a Frenchman with a Flathead wife and one child. The inmates of the next lodge were a halfbreed Iowa, a Nez Perce wife, and two children, his wife's brother and another halfbreed; next lodge was a halfbreed Cree, his wife (a Nez Perce), two children and a Snake Indian. The inmates of the third lodge were a halfbreed Snake, his wife (a Nez Perce), and two children. The remainder were fifteen lodges of Snake Indians. Three of the party spoke English but very broken, therefore that language was made but little use of, as I was familiar with the Canadian French and Indian tongue.

About ten o'clock we sat down to dinner in the lodge where I stayed, which was the most spacious, being about thirty-six feet in circumference at the base, with a fire built in the center. Around this sat on clean epishemores all who claimed kin to the white man (or to use their own expression, all who were gens d'esprit), with their legs crossed in true Turkish style, and now for the dinner.

The first dish that came on was a large tin pan eighteen inches in diameter, rounding full of stewed elk meat. The next dish was similar to the first, heaped up with boiled deer meat (or as the whites would call it, venison, a term not used in the mountains). The third and fourth dishes were equal in size to the first, containing a boiled flour pudding, prepared with dried fruit, accompanied by four quarts of sauce made of the juice of sour berries and sugar. Then came the cakes, followed by about six gallons of strong coffee ready sweetened, with tin cups and pans to drink out of, large chips or pieces of bark supplying the places of plates. On being ready, the butcher knives were drawn and the eating commenced at the word given by the landlady. As all dinners are accompanied by conversation, this was not deficient in that respect. The principal topic which was discussed was the political affairs of the Rocky Mountains, the state of goverements among the different tribes, the personal characters of the most distinguished warrior chiefs, etc. One remarked that the Snake chief, Pahda-hewakunda, was becoming very unpopular and it was the opinion of the Snakes in general that Mohwoom-hah, his brother, would be at the head of affairs before twelve months, as his village already amounted to more than three hundred lodges, and, moreover, he was supported by the bravest men in the nation, among whom were Ink-a-tosh-a-pop, Fibe-bo-un-to-wat-see and Who-sha-kik, who were the pillars of the nation and at whose names the Blackfeet quaked with fear. In like manner were the characters of the principal chiefs of the Bannock, Nez Perce, Flathead, and Crow nations and the policy of their respective nations commented upon by the descendants of Shem and Japhet with as much affected dignity as if they could have read their own names when written, or distinguish the letter B from bull's foot.

Dinner being over, the tobacco pipes were filled and lighted, while the squaws and children cleared away the remains of the feast to one side of the lodge, where they held a sociable tete-a-tete over the fragments. After the pipes were extinguished all agreed to have a frolic shooting at a mark, which occupied the remainder of the day.

CHAPTER XXIX

Solitary Hunting Bouts in the Early Spring of 1841, Near the Great Salt Lake

January 1st—The ground was still bare but the weather cold and the fresh water streams shut up with ice. On the 3d we moved camp up the stream to the foot of the mountain, where the stream forked. The right was called Weaver's Fork and the left Ogden's, both coming through the mountain in a deep narrow cut, The mountain was very high, steep, and rugged. Rising abruptly from the plain about the foot of it were small rolling hills abounding with springs of fresh water. The land bordering on the river and along the stream was a rich, black, alluvial deposit, but the high land was gravelly and covered with wild sage, with here and there a growth of scrubby oaks and red cedars.

On the 10th I started to hunt elk by myself, intending to stop out two or three nights. I traveled up Weaver's Fork in a southeasterly direction through the mountains. The route was very difficult and in many places hard traveling over high points of rocks and around huge precipices, on a trail just wide enough for a single horse to walk. In about ten miles I came into a small plain five or six miles in circumference, just as the sun was setting. Here I stopped for the night. The snow being about five inches deep and the weather cold I made a large fire. As I had not killed any game during the day, I had no supper at night, but I had a blanket, horse to ride and a good rifle with plenty of ammunition and I was not in much danger of suffering by hunger, cold or fatigue, so I wrapped myself in my blanket and laid down on some dry grass I had collected before the fire. About an hour after dark it clouded up and began to snow, but as I was under some large trees it did not trouble me much and I soon fell asleep. At daylight it was still snowing very fast and about eight inches had fallen during the night. I saddled my horse and started in a northerly direction over high, rolling hills covered with scrubby oaks, quaking asps, and maples, for about ten miles, where I came into a smooth valley about twenty miles in circumference, called "Ogden's Hole," with the fork of the same name running through it. Here the snow was about fifteen inches deep on the level. Towards night the weather cleared up and I discovered a band of about 100 elk on the hill among the shrubbery. I approached and killed a very fat old doe, which I butchered and packed the meat and skin on my horse to an open spring about a quarter of a mile distant, where I found plenty of dry wood and where I stopped for the night. I had now a good appetite for supper. After eating I scraped away the snow on one side of the fire, spread down the raw elk hide and laid down, covering myself with my blanket. In the morning when I awoke it was still snowing, and after eating breakfast I packed the meat on my horse and started on foot, leading him by the bridle. Knowing it was impossible to follow down this stream to the plains with a horse, I kept along the foot of the mountain in a northerly direction for about two miles, then turning to the left into a steep ravine began to ascend, winding my way up through the snow, which grew deeper as I ascended. I reached the summit in about three hours. In many places I was obliged to break a trail for my horse. I descended the mountain west to the plains with comparative ease and reached the camp about dark. On arriving at the lodge I entered and sat down before a large, blazing fire. My landlady soon unloaded my horse and turned him loose and then prepared supper, with a good dish of coffee, whilst I, as a matter of course, related the particulars of the hunt. We stayed at this place during the remainder of January. The weather was very cold and the snow about twelve inches deep, but I passed the time agreeably hunting elk among the timber in fair weather and amusing myself with books in foul.

The 2d day of February I took a trip up the mountain to hunt sheep. I ascended a spur with my horse, sometimes riding and then walking, until near the top, where I found a level bench where the wind had blown the snow off. I fastened my horse with a long cord and took along the side of the mountain among the broken crags to see what the chances were for supper. I had not rambled far when, just as the sun was sinking below the dark green waters of the Salt Lake, I discovered three rams about 300 feet perpendicular below me. I shot and killed one of them, but it being so late and the precipice so bad, I concluded to sleep without supper rather than to go after it. I returned to my horse and built a large fire with fragments of dry sugar maple which I found scattered about on the mountain, having for shelter from the wind a huge piece of coarse sand stone of which the mountain was composed. The air was calm, serene, and cold, and the stars shone with an uncommon brightness. After sleeping till midnight I arose and renewed the fire. My horse was continually walking backward and forward to keep from freezing. I was upwards of 6000 feet above the level of the lake. Below me was a dark abyss, silent as the night of death.

I sat and smoked my pipe for about an hour and then laid down and slept until near daylight. My chief object in sleeping at this place was to take a view of the lake when the sun rose in the morning. This range of mountains laid nearly north and south and approached the lake irregularly within from three to ten miles. About eight miles from the southeast shore stood an island about twenty-five miles long and six wide, having the appearance of a low mountain extending north and south and arising 300 or 400 feet above the water. To the north of this about eight miles arose another island, apparently half the size of the first. North of these about six miles and about half way between rose another about six miles in circumference, which appeared to be a mass of basal tic rock with a few scrubby cedars standing about in the cliffs. The others appeared to be clothed with grass and wild sage, but no wood except a few bushes. Near the western horizon arose a small white peak just appearing above the water, which I supposed to be the mountain near the west shore. On the north side a high promontory about six miles wide and ten miles long projected into the lake, covered with grass and scattered cedars. On the south shore rose a vast pile of huge, rough mountains, which I could faintly discern through the dense atmosphere. The water of the lake was too much impregnated with salt to freeze any, even about the shores. About sun an hour high I commenced hunting among the rocks in search of sheep, but did not get a chance to shoot at any till the middle of the afternoon, when crawling cautiously over some shelving cliffs, I discovered ten or twelve ewes feeding some distance below me. I shot and wounded one, reloaded my rifle and crept down to the place I last saw her, when I discovered two standing on the side of a precipice. I shot one through the head and she fell dead on the cliff where she had been standing. I then went above and fastened a cord (which I carried for the purpose) to some bushes which overhung the rock. By this means I descended and rolled her off the cliff where she had caught, and her body fell upwards of 100 feet. I then pulled myself up by the cord and went around the rock down to where she fell, butchered her, hung the meat on a tree, then pursued and killed the other. After butchering the last I took tome of the meat for my supper and started up the mountain and arrived at the place where I had slept about an hour after dark. I soon had a fire blazing and a side of ribs roasting, and procured water by heating stones and melting snow in a piece of skin. By the time supper was over it was late in the night, and I lay down and slept till morning. At sunrise I started on foot to get my meat and left my rifle about half way down the mountain When I came to where the first sheep had been hung in a tree I discovered a large wolverine sitting at the foot of it. I then regretted leaving my rifle, but it was too late, he saw me and took to his heels, as well he might, for he had left nothing behind worth stopping for. All the traces of the sheep I could find were some tufts of hair scattered about the snow. I hunted around for some time, but to no purpose. In the meantime the cautious thief was sitting on the snow at some distance, watching my movements as if he was confident I had no gun and could not find his meat, and wished to aggravate me by his antics. He had made roads in every direction from the foot of the tree, dug holes in the snow in a hundred places apparently to deceive me. I soon got over my ill humor and gave up that a wolverine had fooled a Yankee.

I went to the other sheep and found all safe; carried the meat to my horse, mounted and went to camp.

February 15th—The weather began to moderate and rain and on the 23d the ground was bare about the mountain.

CHAPTER XXX

A Visit to the Eutaw Indian Village—Cordial Treatment at Their Hands

February 24th—I left the camp with a determination to go to the Eutaw village at the southeast extremity of the lake to trade furs I traveled along the foot of the mountain about ten miles, when I stopped and deposited in the ground such articles as I did not wish to take with me. The next day I traveled along the foot of the mountain south, about thirty miles, and encamped on a small spring branch which ran a distance of four miles from the mountain to the lake. This was a beautiful and fertile valley, intersected by large numbers of fine springs which flowed from the mountain to the lake and could, with little labor and expense, be made to irrigate the whole valley. The following day I traveled about fifteen miles along the lake, where a valley opened to my view, stretching to the southeast about forty miles and upward of fifteen miles wide. At the further extremity of this valley laid Trinpan-nah or Eutaw Lake, composed of fresh water, about sixty miles in circumference. The outlet of it was a stream about thirty yards wide, which, after cutting this valley through the middle, emptied into the Salt Lake. I left the lake and traveled up this valley over smooth ground which the snow had long since deserted and the green grass and herbage were fast supplying its place. After Crossing several small streams which intersected this vale, I arrived at the village, rode up to a lodge, and asked of a young Indian who met me where Want-a-Sheep's lodge was; but before he could reply a tall Indian, very dark complected, with a thin visage and a keen, piercing eye, having his buffalo robe thrown carelessly over his left shoulder, gathered in folds around his waist and loosely held by his left hand, stepped forth and answered in the Snake tongue, "I am Want-a-Sheep, follow me," at the same time turning round and directing his course to a large, white lodge. I rode to the door, dismounted and followed him in. He immediately ordered my horses to be unsaddled and turned loose to feed, whilst their loads were carefully arranged in the lodge. After the big pipe had gone around several times in silence, he began the conversation. I was asked the news, where traveling, for what, whom and how. I replied to these general inquiries in the Snake tongue, which was understood by all in the lodge. He then gave me an extract of all he had seen, heard, and done for ten years past. He had two sons and one daughter grown to man and womanhood and the same number of less size. His oldest son was married to a Snake squaw and his daughter to a man of the same nation. The others yet remained single. After supper was over the females retired from the lodge and the principal men assembled to smoke and hear the news, which occupied the time till near midnight, when the assembly broke up, the men retiring to their respective lodges, and the women returned. I passed the time as pleasantly at this place as I ever did among the Indians. In the daytime I rode about the valley hunting wild fowl, which, at this season of the year, rend the air with their cries during the night. The old chief would amuse me with traditional tales, mixed with the grossest superstition, some of which were not unlike the manners of ancient Israelites. There seems to be happiness in ignorance which knowledge and science destroys. Here was a nation of people contented and happy. They had fine horses and lodges and were very partial to the rifles of the white man. If a Eutaw had eight or ten good horses, a rifle, and ammunition, he was contented. If he brought a deer at night from the hunt, joy beamed in the faces of his wife and children and if he returned empty a frown was not seen on the faces of his companions. The buffalo had long since left the shores of these lakes and the hostile Blackfeet had not left a footprint here for many years.

During my stay with these Indians I tried to gain some information respecting the Southern extremity of the Salt Lake, but all that I could learn was that it was a sterile, barren, mountainous country, inhabited by a race of depraved and hostile savages who poisoned their arrows and hindered the exploring of the country.

The chief's son informed me he had come from the largest island in the lake a few days previous, having passed the winter upon it with his family, which he had conveyed back and forth on a raft of bulrushes about twelve-feet square. He said there were large numbers of antelope on the island, and as there was no wood, he had used wild sage for fuel. The old chief told me he could recollect the time when the buffalo passed from the mainland to the island without swimming, and that the depth of the waters was yearly increasing. After obtaining all the furs I could from the Eutaws, I started toward Fort Hall on the 27th of March and traveled along the borders of the lake about twenty-five miles. The fire had run over this part of the country the previous autumn and consumed the dry grass. The new had sprung up to the height of six inches, intermingled with various kinds of flowers in full bloom. The shores of the lake were swarming with water fowl of every species that inhabit inland lakes.

CHAPTER XXXI

Back to Fort Hall—Escorted Missionary to Green River and Back—Old Partners Reunite

The next day I went on to Weaver's River. April 1st I left Weaver's River and traveled along to the northeast extremity of the lake, about twenty-five miles. The next day I went on to Bear River and struck it about fifteen miles below Cache valley and twelve miles from the mouth. There I found my winter comrades and stayed one night and then pursued my journey toward Fort Hall, where I arrived on the 7th of April.

I hunted beaver around the country near the fort until the 15th of June, when the party arrived from the Columbia River, accompanied by a Presbyterian missionary with his wife and one child, on their way to the States. I left the fort with them and conducted them to Green River, where we arrived on the 5th of July. On learning that no party was going to the States, they concluded to return to the Columbia River, and we retraced our steps to Fort Hall, where we arrived on the 8th day of August.

I remained at the fort until the 15th of September, and then started with Elbridge and my old comrade from Vermont to hunt a few more beaver. We went to the headwaters of Blackfoot, where we stayed ten days and then crossed the mountain in a southwest direction on to Bear River, which we struck about twenty-five miles below the Snake Lake. We continued hunting beaver and antelope between this place and the Soda Springs until the 10th of October. We then traveled down Bear River to Cache valley, where we stopped until the 21st, then we followed down the river near where it empties into the Salt Lake. Along the bank of this stream for about ten miles from the lake extends a barren, clay flat, destitute of vegetation excepting a few willows along the bank of the river and scattering spots of salt grass and sage. In one place there was about four or five acres covered about four inches deep with the most beautiful salt I have ever seen. Two crusts had formed, one at the bottom and the other on the top, which has protected it from being the least bit soiled. Between those crusts the salt was completely dry, loose, and composed of very small grains of a snowy whiteness.

We stopped about this place until the 5th of November and then returned to Fort Hall, where, after remaining a few days, we concluded to go on to the head streams of Portneuf and stop until the waters froze up. We traveled up about forty miles and arranged an encampment in a beautiful valley, as the weather began to grow cold.

In the year 1836 large bands of buffalo could be seen in almost every little valley on the small branches of this stream. At this time the only traces of them which could be seen were the scattered bones of those which had been killed. Their deeply indented trails which had been made in former years were overgrown with grass and weeds. The trappers often remarked to each other as they rode over these lonely plains that it was time for the white man to leave the mountains, as beaver and game had nearly disappeared.

On the 15th of November I started up a high mountain in search of sheep. After hunting and scrambling over the rocks for half a day without seeing any traces of sheep I sat down upon a rock which overlooked the country below me. At length, casting a glance along the south side of the mountain, I discovered a large grizzly bear sitting at the mouth of his den. I approached within about 180 paces, shot, and missed him. He looked around and crept slowly into his den. I reloaded my rifle, went up to the hole and threw down a stone weighing five or six pounds, which soon rattled to the bottom and I heard no more. I then rolled a stone weighing 300 or 400 pounds into the den, stepped back two or three steps and prepared myself for the outcome. The stone had scarcely reached the bottom when the bear came rushing out, with his mouth wide open, and was on the point of making a spring at me when I pulled trigger and shot him through the left shoulder, which sent him rolling down the mountain. It being near night, I butchered him and left the meat lying and returned to camp. The next day I took the meat to camp, where we salted and smoked it, ready for winter's use. We stopped about on these streams until the 15th of December, then returned to Fort Hall, where we stayed until the 24th of March. The winter was unusually severe. The snow was fifteen inches deep over the valley after settling and becoming hard. We had no thawing weather until the 18th of March, when it began to rain and continued for four days and nights, which drove the snow nearly all from the plains.

CHAPTER XXXII

Closing Incidents of an Interesting Experience—The Author Leaves the Mountains for Oregon

March 25th—I started, in company with Alfred Shutes, my old comrade from Vermont, to go to the Salt Lake and pass the spring hunting water fowl, eggs, and beaver. We left the fort and traveled in a southerly direction to the mountain, about thirty miles. The next day we traveled south about fifteen miles through a low defile and the day following we crossed the divide and fell on to a stream called "Malade" or Sick River, which empties into Bear River about ten miles from the mouth. This stream takes its name from the beaver which inhabit it living on poison roots. Those who eat their meat become sick at the stomach in a few hours and the whole system is filled with cramps and severe pains, but I have never known or heard of a person dying with the disease. We arrived at the mouth of Bear River on the 2d of April. Here we found the ground dry, the grass green and myriads of swans, geese, brants, and ducks, which kept up a continual hum day and night, assisted by the uncouth notes of the sand hill cranes. The geese, ducks, and swans are very fat at this season of the year. We caught some few beaver and feasted on fowls and eggs until the 20th of May and returned to the fort, where we stopped until the 20th of June, when a small party arrived from the mouth of the Columbia River on their way to the United States, and my comrade made up his mind once more to visit his native Green Mountains, after an absence of sixteen years, while I determined on going to the mouth of the Columbia and settle myself in the Willamette or Multnomah valley. I accompanied my comrade up Ross Fork about twenty-five miles on his journey and the next morning, after taking an affectionate leave of each other, I started to the mountains for the purpose of killing elk and drying meat for my journey to the Willamette valley. I ascended to the top of Ross mountain (on which the snows remain till the latter part of August), sat down under a pine and took a last farewell view of a country over which I had traveled so often under such a variety of circumstances. The recollections of the past, connected with the scenery now spread out before me, put me somewhat in a poetical humor, and for the first time I attempted to frame my thoughts into rhyme, but if poets will forgive me for this intrusion I shall be cautious about trespassing on their grounds in future.

In the evening I killed an elk and on the following day cured the meat for packing. From thence I returned to the fort, where I stayed till the 22d of August.

In the meantime there arrived at the fort a party of emigrants from the States, on their way to the Oregon country, among whom was Dr. E. White, United States sub-agent for the Oregon Indians. 23d—I started with them and arrived at the falls of the Willamette river on the 26th day of September, 1842.

It would be natural for me to suppose that after escaping all the dangers attendant upon nearly nine years' residence in a wild, inhospitable region like the Rocky Mountains, where I was daily, and a great part of the time, hourly, anticipating danger from hostile savages and other sources, I should, on arriving in a civilized and an enlightened community, live in comparative security, free from the harassing intrigues of Dame Fortune's eldest daughter, but I found it was all a delusion, for danger is not always the greatest when most apparent, as will appear in the sequel.

On arriving at the Falls of the Willamette, I found a number of Methodist missionaries and American farmers had formed themselves into a company for the purpose of erecting mills and a sawmill was then building on an island standing on the brink of the falls, which went into operation about two months after I arrived. In the meantime, Dr. John McLoughlin, a chief factor of the Hudson Bay Company, who contemplated leaving the service of the company and permanently settling with his family and fortune in the Willamette valley, laid off a town (the present Oregon City) on the east side of the falls and began erecting a sawmill on a site he had prepared some years previous by cutting a race through the rock to let the water on to his works when they should be constructed.

The following spring the American company commenced building a flour mill and I was employed to assist in its construction. On the 6th day of June I was engaged with the contractor in blasting some points of rock in order to sink the water sill to its proper place, when a blast exploded accidentally by the concussion of small particles of rock near the powder, a piece of rock weighing about sixty pounds struck me on the right side of the face and knocked me, senseless, six feet backward.

I recovered my senses in a few minutes and was assisted to walk to my lodgings. Nine particles of rock of the size of wild goose shot each had penetrated my right eye and destroyed it forever. The contractor escaped with the loss of two fingers of his left hand.

THE HUNTER'S FAREWELL

Adieu, ye hoary, icy-mantled towers,
      That ofttimes pierce the onward fleeting mists,
Whose feet are washed by gentle summer showers,
      While Phoebus' rays play on your sparkling crests;
The smooth, green vales you seem prepared to guard,
      Beset with groves of ever-verdant pine,
Would furnish themes for Albion's noble bards,
      Far 'bove a hunter's rude, unvarnish'd rhyme.

Adieu, ye flocks that skirt the mountain's brow
      And sport on banks of everlasting snow,
Ye timid lambs and simple, harmless ewes,
      Who fearless view the dread abyss below;
Oft have I watched your seeming mad career
      While lightly tripping o'er those dismal heights,

Or cliffs o'erhanging yawning caverns drear,
    Where none else tread save fowls of airy flight.

Oft have I climbed these rough, stupendous rocks
    In search of food 'mongst Nature's well-fed herds,
Until I've gained the rugged mountain's top,
    Where Boreas reigned or feathered monarch soar'd;
On some rude crag projecting from the ground
    I've sat a while my wearied limbs to rest,
And scanned the unsuspecting flocks around
    With anxious care selecting out the best.

The prize obtained, with slow and heavy step
    Pac'd down the steep and narrow winding path,
To some smooth vale where crystal streamlets met,
    And skillful hands prepared a rich repast;
Then hunters' jokes and merry humor'd sport
    Beguiled the time, enlivened every face,
The hours flew fast and seemed like moments, short,
    'Til twinkling planets told of midnight's pace.

But now those scenes of cheerful mirth are done,
    The antlered herds are dwindling very fast,
The numerous trails so deep by bison worn,
    Now teem with weeds or overgrown with grass;
A few gaunt wolves now scattered o'er the place
    Where herds, since time unknown to man, have fed,

With lonely howls and sluggish, onward pace,
    Tell their sad fate and where their bones are laid.

Ye rugged mounts, ye vales, ye streams and trees,
    To you a hunter bids his last farewell,
I'm bound for shores of distant western seas,
    To view far-famed Multnomah's fertile vale;
I'll leave these regions, once famed hunting grounds,
    Which I, perhaps, again shall see no more,
And follow down, led by the setting sun,
    Or distant sound of proud Columbia's roar.

June 22,1842.   —OSBORNE RUSSELL.

APPENDIX

It has been my design whilst keeping a journal to note down the principal circumstances which came under my immediate observation as I passed along, and I have mostly deferred giving a general description of Indians and animals that inhabit the Rocky Mountains until the last end in order that I might be able to put the information I have collected in a more compact form. I have been very careful in gathering information from the most intelligent Indians and experienced white hunters, but have excluded from this journal such parts (with few exceptions) as I have not proved true by experience. I am fully aware of the numerous statements which have been given to travelers in a jocular manner by the hunters and traders among the Rocky Mountains, merely to hear themselves talk, or according to the mountaineers' expression, give them a long yarn or "fish story" to put in their journals, and I have frequently seen those "fish stories" published with the original very much enlarged which had not at first the slightest ground for truth to rest upon. It is utterly impossible for a person who is merely traveling through or even residing one or two years in the Rocky Mountains to give an accurate description of the country or its inhabitants.

I have never known but one Rocky Mountaineer to keep a regular journal, and he could not have visited the northern part of them, as I am confident his compiler (Mr. Flint) would not knowingly be led into such errors as occur in James O'Pattie's Journal, both in regard to the location of the country and Indians inhabiting the northern section of it. He says, "The Flathead nation of Indians flatten their heads and live between the Platte and Yellowstone Rivers," which is not, nor ever was, the case in either instance. He also says that Lewis River and the Arkansas head near each other in Long's Peak. I never was at Long's Peak or the head of the Arkansas River, but am fully confident can be within 300 miles of the source of Lewis's River. These are among the numerous errors which I discovered in reading James O'Pattie's Journal, embellished by Mr. Flint of Cincinnati. These are among the reasons for which I offer this to public view, hoping that it not only may be of interest to myself but the means of correcting some erroneous statements which have gone forth to the world, unintentionally perhaps by their authors.

THE WOLVERINE, CARCAJOU, OR GLUTTON

This species of animal is very numerous in the Rocky Mountains and very mischievous and annoying to the hunters. They often get into the traps setting for beaver or search out the deposits of meat which the weary hunter has made during a toilsome day's hunt among mountains too rugged and remote for him to bear the reward of his labours to the place of encampment, and when finding these deposits the carcajou carries off all or as much of the contents as he is able, secreting it in different places among the snow, rock, or bushes in such a manner that it is very difficult for man or beast to find it. The avaricious disposition of this animal has given rise to the name of glutton by naturalists, who suppose that it devours so much at a time as to render it stupid and incapable of moving or running about, but I have never seen an instance of this kind; on the contrary I have seen them quite expert and nimble immediately after having carried away four to five times their weight in meat. I have good reason to believe that the carcajou's appetite is easily satisfied upon meat freshly killed, but after it becomes putrid it may become more voracious, but I never saw one myself or a person who had seen one in a stupid, dormant state caused by glutting, although I have often wished it were the case.

The body is thick and long, the legs short, the feet and claws are longer in proportion than those of the black bear, which it very much resembles, with the exception of its tail, which is twelve inches long and bushy. Its body is about three feet long and stands fifteen inches high; its color is black excepting the sides, which are of a dirty white or light brown.

Its movements are somewhat quicker than those of the bear and it climbs trees with ease. I have never known, either by experience or information, the carcajou to prey upon animals of its own killing larger than very young fawns or lambs, although it has been described by naturalists and generally believed that it climbs trees and leaps down upon elk, deer, and other large animals and clings to their back till it kills them in spite of their efforts to get rid of it by speed or resistance, but we need go no further than the formation of the animal to prove those statements erroneous. Its body, legs, feet, and mouth are shaped similarly to the black bear, as has been already stated, but its claws are somewhat longer and stronger in proportion, and like the bear, its claws are somewhat blunted at the points, which would render it impossible for them to cling to the back of an elk or deer while running. I do not pretend to say, however, what may be its habits in other countries, I only write from experience. They do not den up like the bear in winter, but ramble about the streams among the high mountains, where they find springs open. Its hair is three inches long and in the summer is coarse like the bear, but winter it is near as fine as that of the red fox. The female brings forth its young in April and generally brings two at a birth.

THE WOLF

Of this species of animal there are several kinds, as the buffalo wolf, the big prairie wolf, and the small prairie or medicine wolf. The buffalo wolf is from two to three feet high and from four to five feet long from the tip of his nose to the insertion of the tail. Its hair is long, coarse, and shaggy. Its color varies from a dark grey to a snowy whiteness. They are not ferocious toward man and will run at the sight of him. The big prairie wolf is two feet high and three and a half feet long; its hair is long and shaggy, its color is a dirty grey, often inclining to a brown or brindle. The least known is little prairie or medicine wolf. Its size is somewhat larger than the red fox; its color is brownish grey and its species something between the big wolf and the fox. The Indians are very superstitious about this animal. When it comes near a village and barks they say there is people near. Some pretend to distinguish between its warning the approach of friends or enemies and in the latter case I have often seen them secure their horses and prepare themselves to fight. I have often seen this prophecy tolerably accurately fulfilled and again I have as often seen it fail, but a superstitious Indian will always account for the failure.

The habits of these three kinds of wolves are similar. Their rutting season is in March. The female brings forth from two to six at a birth.

THE PANTHER

This animal is rarely seen in the plains, but confines itself to the more woody and mountainous districts. Its color is light brown on the back and the belly is a sort of ash color; its length is five feet from the tip of the nose to the insertion of the tail, which is about one-half the length of the body. It is very destructive on sheep and other animals that live in the high mountains, but will run at the sight of a man and has a great antipathy to fire.

THE MARMOT

This animal inhabits the rocks and precipices of the highest mountains. Its color is a dark brown, its size less than the smallest rabbit; its ears and paws are shaped like those of the rat, and its cry resembles that of the bleating of the young lambs. During the summer it collects large quantities of hay and mud with which it secures its habitation from the cold during the winter. On my first acquaintance with this animal I was led to suppose that the hay which they accumulate in summer was calculated to supply them with food during the winter, but this I found to be erroneous by visiting their habitation in the early part of spring and finding their stock in nowise diminished. I have good reason to suppose that they lie dormant during the winter.

THE PORCUPINE

This species of animal is too well known to need a minute description in this place. They are, however, very numerous and their flesh is much esteemed by some of the Indian tribes for food, and their quills are held in the highest estimation by all for embroidering their dresses, and other functions, which is done with peculiar elegance and uncommon skill. It subsists chiefly on the bark of trees and other vegetables.

THE BADGER

This species of animal are numerous in the Rocky Mountains. Their skins are much used by the Snake and Bannock Indians for clothing, as well as their flesh for food. They make their habitation in the ground in the most extensive plains and are found ten miles from water.

THE GROUND HOG

These animals are also very numerous and their skins much used by the Indians for clothing in sections of country where deer and buffalo are not to be found. They are not so large as the ground hog of the United States, but are in all respects the same species. They live among the rocks near streams and feed upon grass and other vegetables. The shrill cry with which their sentinels give warning of danger resembles that of the United States species.

THE GRIZZLY BEAR

Much has been said by travelers in regard to this animal, yet while giving a description of animals that inhabit the Rocky Mountains, I do not feel justified in simply passing over in silence the most ferocious species without undertaking to contribute some little information respecting it which, although it may not be important, I hope some of it at least will be new. It lives chiefly upon roots and berries, being of too slow a nature to live much upon game of its own killing, and from May to September it never tastes flesh. The rutting season is in November and the female brings forth from one to three at a birth. I have not been able to ascertain the precise time that the female goes with young, but I suppose from experience and inquiry it is about fourteen weeks. The young are untameable and manifest a savage ferocity when scarcely old enough to crawl. Several experiments have been tried in the Rocky Mountains for taming them, but to no effect. They are possessed of great muscular strength. I have seen a female, which was wounded by a rifle ball in the loins so as to disable her, kill her young with one stroke of her forepaws as fast as they approached her. If a young cub is wounded and commences making a noise, the mother invariably springs upon it and kills it. When grown they never make a noise except a fearful growl. They get to be fatter than any other animals in the Rocky Mountains during the season when wild fruit is abundant. The flesh of the grizzly bear is preferable to pork. It lives in winter in caves in the rocks or holes dug in the ground on high ridges. It loses no flesh while confined to its den during the winter, but is equally as fat in the spring when it leaves the den as when it enters it at the beginning of the winter. There is seldom to be found more than one in a den excepting the female and her young. I have seen them measure seven feet from the tip of the nose to the insertion of the tail. It will generally run from the scent of a man, but when it does not get the scent it will often let him approach close enough to spring on him and when wounded it is a dangerous animal to trifle with. Its speed is comparatively slow down hill but much greater in ascending. It never climbs trees, as its claws are too straight for that purpose.

THE BLACK BEAR

The black bear of the mountains are much the same species as those of the States. In comparison with the grizzly it is entirely harmless. It is seldom found in the plains, but inhabits the timbered and mountainous districts. They are not very numerous and their habits are too well known to need a detailed description here.

THE MOUNTAIN SHEEP OR BIG HORN

These animals answer somewhat to the description given by naturalists of the musmon or wild sheep which are natives of Greece, Corsica, and Tartary. The male and female very much resemble the domestic ram and ewe, but are much larger. The horns of the male are much larger in proportion to the body than the domestic rams, but those of the females are almost in the same proportion to the domestic ewe. In the month of May, after they have shed their old coat and the new one appears, their color is dark blue or mouse color, except the extremity of the rump and hinder parts of the thighs, which are white. As the season advances and the hair grows long it gradually turns or fades to a dirty brown. In the month of December the hair is about three inches long, thickly matted together, rendering it impenetrable to the cold. Its hair is similar in texture to that of the deer, and like the latter it is short and smooth upon its forehead and legs. They inhabit the highest and most craggy mountains and never descend to the plains unless compelled by necessity. In the winter season the snow drives them down to the low craggy mountains facing the south, but in the spring as the snow begins to recede they follow it, keeping close to where the grass is short and tender. Its speed on the smooth ground is slower than the deer, but in climbing steep rocks or precipices it is almost incredible, insomuch that the wolf, lynx and panther give up the chase whenever the sheep reach the rugged crags.

The fearful height from which it jumps and the small points on which it alights without slipping or missing its footing is astonishing to its pursuers, whether man or beast. Its hoofs are very hard and pointed and it reposes upon the most bleak points of rock both in summer and winter. The male is a noble looking animal as he stands upon an elevated point with his large horns curling around his ears like the coil of a serpent, and his head held proudly erect, disdaining the lower regions and its inhabitants. Its flesh has a similar taste to mutton, but its flavor is more agreeable and the meat more juicy. Their rutting season is in November, when the rams have furious battles with each other in the same manner as the domestic rams. The victor often knocks his opponent over a high precipice when he is dashed to pieces in the fall. The sound of their heads coming in contact is often heard a mile distant. The female produces from one to three at a birth. The lambs are of a whitish color, very innocent and playful. Hunting sheep is often attended with great danger, especially in the winter season, when the rocks and precipices are covered with snow and ice, but the excitement created by hunting them often enables the hunter to surmount obstacles which at other times would seem impossible. The skins, when dressed are finer, softer and far superior to those of the deer for clothing. It is of them that the squaws make their dresses which they embroider with beads and porcupine quills dyed with various colors, which are wrought into figures displaying a tolerable degree of taste and ingenuity.

THE GAZELLE OR MOUNTAIN ANTELOPE

This animal, for beauty and fleetness, surpasses all the ruminating animals of the Rocky Mountains. Its body is rather smaller than the common deer; its color on the back and upper part of the sides is light brown, the hinder part of the thighs and belly are white, the latter having a yellowish cast. The under part of the neck is white with several black stripes running across the throat down to the breast. Its legs are very slim, neat and small. Its ears are black on the inside and around the edges with the remainder brown. Its horns are also black and flattened; the horns of the males are much longer than those of the females, but formed in the same manner; they project up about eight inches on the males and then divide into two branches, the one inclining backward and the other forward with sometimes an additional branch coming out near the head inclining inward. The two upper branches are six inches long, the hindermost forming a sort of hook. The nose is black and a strip of the same color runs round under the eyes and terminates under the ears. It runs remarkably smooth and in the summer season the fleetest horses but rarely overtake it. Its natural walk is stately and elegant, but it is very timid and fearful and can see to a great distance, but with all its timidity and swiftness of foot its curiosity often leads it to destruction. If it discovers anything of a strange appearance (particularly anything red) it goes direct to it and will often approach within thirty paces. They are very numerous in the plains, but seldom found among timber. Their flesh is similar to venison. The female produces two at a birth and the young are suckled until a month old. They are easily domesticated.

THE BLACK-TAILED DEER

This animal is somewhat larger than the common deer of the United States. Its ears are very long, from which it has derived the appellation of mule deer. Its color in summer is red, but in the latter part of August its hair turns to a deep blue ground with about half an inch of white on each hair one-fourth inch from the outer ends, which presents a beautiful grey color. It lives among the mountains and seldom descends among the plains. Its flesh is similar in every respect to the common deer. The tail is about six inches long and the hair upon it smooth except upon the end, where there is a small tuft of black. The female goes six months with young and generally produces two at a birth. The young is brought forth in April and remains in an almost helpless state for one month. During its state of inability the mother secretes it in some secure place in the long grass and weeds, where it remains contented while she often wanders half a mile from it in search of food. The color of the fawn is red intermingled with white spots, and it is generally believed by Indians that so long as those spots remain (which is about two and one-half months) that no beast of prey can scent them. This I am inclined to believe, as I have often seen wolves pass very near the place where fawns were lying without stopping or altering their course, and were it not for some secret provision of nature, the total annihilation of this species of animal would be inevitable in those countries infested by wolves and other beasts of prey as in the Rocky Mountains. This safeguard is given by the Great Founder of Nature, not only to the black tailed deer but all of the species, including elk and antelope, whose young are so spotted at their birth. I do not consider that the mere white spots are a remedy against their scent of wild beasts, but they mark the period of inability, for when these disappear the little animals are capable of eluding their pursuers by flight. The male, like the common deer, drops its horns in February. It then cannot be distinguished from the former except by its larger size.

THE RABBIT

This species of animal is very numerous and various in their sizes and colors. The large hares of the plains are very numerous, the common sized rabbits are equally or more numerous than the others, and there is also the small brown rabbit which does not change its color during the winter season as do the others, but the most singular kind is the black rabbit. It is a native of mountainous forests. Its color is coal black excepting two small white spots which are on the throat and lower part of the belly. In winter its color is milk white. Its body is about the size of the common rabbit with the exception of its ears, which are much longer. Another kind is the black-tailed rabbit of the plains. It is rather larger than the common rabbit and derives its name from the color of its tail, which never changes its color.

THE ELK

This animal is eight feet long from the tip of the nose to the insertion of the tail, and stands four and one-half feet high. Its proportions are similar to those of the deer, except the tail, which is four inches long and composed of a black gummy substance intermingled with fibers around the bone, the whole being clothed with skin and covered with hair like the body. Its color in summer is red but in winter is a brownish grey except the throat and belly, the former being dark brown and the latter white inclining to yellow, extending to the hind part of the thighs as far as the insertion of the tail. They are very timid and harmless even when so disabled as to render escape impossible. Its speed is very swift when running single, but when running in large bands they soon become wearied by continual collision with each other, and if they are closely pressed by the hunter on horseback they soon commence dropping down flat on the ground to elude their pursuers and will suffer themselves to be killed with a knife in this position. When the band is first located the hunters keep at some distance behind to avoid dispersing them, and to frighten them the more a continual noise is kept up by halloing and shooting over them, which causes immediate confusion and collision of the band and the weakest elk soon begin to fall to the ground exhausted. Their rutting time is in September, when they collect in immense bands among the timber along the streams and among the mountains. It has been stated by naturalists that the male is a very formidable and dangerous animal when pursued, but I never saw it act on the offensive, neither have I ever known one to offer resistance in defense of itself against man otherwise than by involuntary motions of its head or feet when too much disabled to rise from the ground. I have often seen the female come about the hunter who has found where her young is secreted uttering the most pitiful and persuasive moans and pleading in the most earnest manner that a dumb brute is capable of for the life of her young. This mode of persuasion would, I think, excite sympathy in the breast of any human that was not entirely destitute of the passion.

The fawn has a peculiar cry after it is able to run which resembles the first scream of a child, by which it answers the dam, who calls it by a note similar to the scream of a woman in distress.

In the month of September the males have a peculiar shrill call which commences in a piercing whistle and ends in a coarse gurgling in the throat. By this they call the females to assemble and each other to the combat, in which by their long antlers they are rendered formidable to each other. The hair stands erect and the head is lowered to give or receive the attack, but the victor seldom pursues the vanquished.

THE BUFFALO OR BISON

This animal has been so minutely described by travelers that I have considered it of little importance to enter into the details of its shape and size, and shall therefore omit those descriptions with which I suppose the public to be already acquainted, and try to convey some idea of its peculiarities which probably are not so well known. The vast numbers of these animals which once traversed such an extensive region on North America are diminishing. The continued increasing demand for robes in the civilized world has already and is still contributing in no small degree to their destruction, whilst on the other hand the continued increase of wolves and other four-footed enemies far exceeds that of the buffaloes. When these combined efforts for their destruction are taken into consideration, it will not be doubted for a moment that this noble race of animals, so useful in supplying the wants of man, will at no far distant period become extinct in North America. The buffalo is already a stranger, although so numerous ten years ago, in that part of the country which is drained by the sources of the Colorado, Bear, and Snake Rivers, and occupied by the Snake and Bannock Indians. The flesh of the buffalo cow is considered far superior to that of the domestic beef and it is so much impregnated with salt that it requires but little seasoning when cooked. All the time, trouble, and care bestowed by man upon improving the breed and food of meat cattle seems to be entirely thrown away when we compare those animals in their original state which are reared upon the food supplied them by nature with the same species when domesticated and fed on cultivated grasses and grains, and the fact seems to justify the opinion that nature will not allow herself to be outdone by art, for it is fairly proven in this enlightened age that the rude and untaught savage feasts on better beef and mutton than the most learned and experienced agriculturists. Now if every effect is produced by a cause, perhaps I may stumble upon the cause which produces the effect in this instance. At any rate I shall attempt it:

In the first place, the rutting season of the buffaloes is regular, commencing about the 15th of July when the males and females are fat, and ends about the 15th of August. Consequently the females bring forth their young in the latter part of April and the first of May, when the grass is most luxuriant and thereby enables the cow to afford the most nourishment for her calf and enables the young to quit the natural nourishment of its dam and feed upon the tender herbage sooner than it would at any other season of the year. Another proof is the fact that when the rutting season commences the strongest, healthiest, and most vigorous bulls drive the weaker ones from the cows, hence the calves are from the best breed, which is thereby kept upon a regular basis. In the summer season they generally go to water and drink once in twenty-four hours, but in the winter they seldom get water at all. The cows are fattest in October and the bulls in July. The cows retain their flesh in a great measure throughout the winter until the spring opens and they get at water, from whence they become poor in a short time. So much for the regularity of their habits, and the next point is the food on which they subsist. The grass on which the buffaloes generally feed is short, firm and of the most nutritious kind. The salts with which the mountain regions are impregnated are imbibed in a great degree by the vegetation and as there is very little rain in summer, autumn, or winter, the grass arrives at maturity and dries in the sun without being cut it is made like hay; in this state it remains throughout the winter and while the spring rains are divesting the old growth of its nutritive qualities they are in the meantime pushing forward the new. The buffaloes are very particular in their choice of grass, always preferring the short of the uplands to that of the luxuriant growth of the fertile alluvial bottoms. Thus they are taught by nature to choose such food as is most palatable and she has also provided that such as is most palatable is the best suited to their condition and that condition the best calculated to supply the wants and necessities of her rude, untutored children for whom they were prepared. Thus nature looks with a smile of derision upon the magnified efforts of art to excel her works by a continual breach of her laws.

The most general mode practiced by Indians for killing buffalo is running upon horseback and shooting them with arrows, but it requires a degree of experience for both man and horse to kill them in this manner with any degree of safety, particularly in places where the ground is rocky and uneven. The horse that is well trained for this purpose not only watches the ground over which he is running and avoids the holes, ditches and rocks by shortening or extending his leaps, but also the animal which he is pursuing in order to prevent being "horned" when 'tis brought suddenly to bay, which is done instantaneously, and if the buffalo wheel to the right the horse passes as quick as thought to the left behind it and thereby avoids its horns; but if the horse in close pursuit wheels on the same side with the buffalo he comes directly in contact with its horns and with one stroke the horse's entrails are often torn out and his rider thrown headlong to the ground. After the buffalo is brought to bay the trained horse will immediately commence describing a circle about ten paces from the animal in which he moves continuously in a slow gallop or trot which prevents the raging animal from making a direct bound at him by keeping it continuously turning around until it is killed by the rider with arrows or bullets. If a hunter discovers a band of buffalo in a place too rough and broken for his horse to run with safety and there is smooth ground near by, he secretly rides on the leeward side as near as he can without being discovered. He then starts up suddenly without apparently noticing the buffalo and gallops in the direction he wishes the band to run. The buffalo, on seeing him run to the plain, start in the same direction in order to prevent themselves from being headed and kept from the smooth ground. The same course would be pursued if he wished to take them to any particular place in the mountains. One of the hunters' first instructions to an inexperienced hand is "run toward the place where you wish the buffalo to run but do not close on them behind until they get to that place." For instance, if the hunter is to the right, the leading buffaloes keep inclining to the right and if he should fall in behind and crowd upon the rear they would separate in different directions and it would be a mere chance if any took the direction he wished them. When he gets to the plain he gives his horse the rein and darts through the band, selects his victim, reins his horse alongside, and shoots, and if he considers the wound mortal, he pulls up the rein, the horse, knowing his business, keeps along galloping with the band until the rider has reloaded when he darts forward upon another buffalo as at first. A cow seldom stops at bay after she is wounded, and therefore is not so dangerous as a bull, who wheels soon after he is pushed from the band and becomes fatigued, whether he is wounded or not. When running over ground where there are rocks, holes, or gullies, the horse must be reined up gradually if he is reined at all. There is more accidents happen in running buffalo by the riders getting frightened and suddenly checking their horses than any other way. If they come upon a coulee which the horse can leap by an extra exertion the best plan is to give him the rein and the whip or spur at the same time and fear not, for any ditch that a buffalo can leap can be cleared with safety by a horse and one too wide for a buffalo to clear an experienced rider will generally see in time to check his horse gradually before he gets to it. And now, as I have finished my description of the buffaloes and the manner of killing them, I wish put a simple question for the reader's solution:

If kings, princes, nobles, and gentlemen can derive so much sport and pleasure as they boast of in chasing a fox or simple hare all day, which when they have caught is of no use to them, what pleasure can the Rocky Mountain hunter be expected to derive in running with a well trained horse such a noble and stately animal as the bison, which when killed is of some service to him? There are men of noble birth, noble estates, and noble minds who have attained to a tolerable degree of perfection in fox hunting in Europe and buffalo hunting in the Rocky Mountains, and I have heard some of them decide that the points would not bear a comparison if the word "fashion" could be stricken from the English language.

It also requires a considerable degree of practice to approach on foot and kill buffalo with a rifle. A person must be well acquainted with the shape and make of the animal and the manner in which it is standing in order to direct his aim with certainty. And it also requires experience to enable him to choose a fat animal. The best looking buffalo is not always the fattest and a hunter by constant practice may lay down rules for selecting the fattest when on foot which would be no guide to him when running upon horseback, for he is then placed in a different position and one which requires different rules for choosing.

THE BEAVER

The beaver, as almost every one knows, is an amphibious animal, but the instinct with which it is possessed surpasses the reason of a no small portion of the human race. Its average size is about two and one-half feet long from the point of the nose to the insertion of the tail, which is from ten to fifteen inches long and from five to nine broad, flat in the shape of a spade rounded at the corners and covered with a thick, rough skin resembling scales. The tail serves the double purpose of steering and assisting it through the water by a quick up and down motion. The hind feet are webbed and the toe next the outside on each has a double nail which serves the purpose of a toothpick to extract the splinters of wood from their teeth. As they are the only animals that cut large trees for subsistence, they are also the only animals known to be funished with nails so peculiarly adapted to the purpose for which they are used. Its color is of a light brown generally, but I have seen them of a jet black frequently, and in one instance I saw one of a light cream color having the feet and tail white. The hair is of two sorts, the one longer and coarser, the other fine, short and silky. The teeth are like those of the rat but are longer and stronger in proportion to the size of the animals. To a superficial observer they have but one vent for their excrements and urine, but upon a closer examination without dissection separate openings will be seen, likewise four gland openings forward of the arms, two containing oil with which they oil their coats, the others containing the castorium, a collection of gummy substance of a yellow color which is extracted from the food of the animal and conveyed through small vessels into the glands. It is this deposit which causes the destruction of the beaver by the hunters. When a beaver, male or female, leaves the lodge to swim about their pond, they go to the bottom and fetch up some mud between their forepaws and breast, carry it on the bank and emit upon it a small quantity of castorium. Another beaver passing the place does the same, and should a hundred beaver pass within the scent of the place, they would each throw up mud covering up the old castorium and emit new upon that which they had thrown up. The trapper extracts this substance from the gland and carries it in a wooden box. He sets his trap in the water near the bank about six inches below the surface, throws a handful of mud upon the bank about one foot from it and puts a small portion of the castorium thereon. After night the beaver comes out of his lodge, smells the fatal bait 200 or 300 yards distant and steers his course directly for it. He hastens to ascend the bank, but the trap grasps his foot and soon drowns him in the struggle to escape, for the beaver, though termed an amphibious animal, cannot respire beneath the water.

The female brings forth her young in April and produces from two to six at a birth, but what is most singular, she seldom raises but two, a male and a female. This peculiarity of the beaver has often been a matter of discussion among the most experienced of hunters, whether the dam or father kills the young, but I have come to the conclusion that it is the mother for the following reasons: First, the male is seldom found about the lodge for ten or fifteen days after the female brings forth; second, there is always a male and female saved alive; third, I have seen the dead kittens floating in the ponds freshly killed and at the same time have caught the male when he was living more than one-half mile from the lodge.

I have found, where beaver are confined to a limited space, they kill nearly all the kittens, which is supposed to be done to keep them from becoming too numerous and destroying the timber and undergrowth too fast. I have caught fifty full grown beaver in a valley surrounded by mountains and cascades where they had not been disturbed for four years and with this number there were but five or six kittens and yearlings. The young ones pair off generally at three years of age to set up for themselves and proceed up or down a stream as instinct may suggest until they find the best place for wood and undergrowth connected with the most convenient place for building a dam, which is constructed by cutting small trees and brush, dragging them into the water on both sides of the stream, and attaching one end to each bank, while the other extends into the stream inclining upward against the current. Then mud, small stones and rubbish are dragged or pushed onto it to sink it to the bottom. They proceed in this manner till the two ends meet in the middle of the stream, the whole forming a sort of curved line across, but the water raising often forces the dam down the stream until it becomes nearly straight. In the meantime they have selected a spot for the lodge either upon the bank or upon a small island formed by the rising water, but it is generally constructed on an island in the middle of the pond with sticks and mud in such a manner that when the water is raised sufficiently high, which generally is from four to seven feet, it has the appearance of a potash kettle turned on the surface bottom upwards, standing from four to six feet above the water. There is no opening above the water, but generally two below. The floor on which they sleep and have their beds of straw or grass, is about twelve inches above the water level. The room is arched over and kept neat and clean. When the leaves begin to fall, the beavers commence laying in their winter store. They often cut down trees from twelve to eighteen inches in diameter and cut off the branches covered with smooth bark into pieces from two to six feet long. These they drag into the water, float them to the lodge, sink them to the bottom of the pond, and there fasten them. In this manner they proceed until they have procured about half a cord of wood, solid measure, for each beaver's winter supply. By this time the dam freezes over and all is shut up with ice. The beaver has nothing to do but leap into the water through the subterranean passage and bring up a stick of wood which is to furnish him his meal. This he drags up by one end into the lodge, eats off the bark to a certain distance, then cuts off the part he has stripped and throws it into the water through another passage, and so proceeds until he has finished his meal. When the ice and snow disappears in the spring, they clear their pond of the stripped wood and stop the leaks which the frosts have occasioned in their dam. Their manner of enlarging their lodge is by cutting out the inside and adding more to the out. The covering of the lodge is generally about eighteen inches thick, formed by sticks and mud intermingled in such a manner that it is very difficult for man, beast or cold to penetrate through it.

THE SNAKE INDIANS

The appellation by which this nation is distinguished is derived from the Crows, but from what reason I have never been able to determine. They call themselves Sho-sho-nies, but during an acquaintance of nine years, during which time I made further progress in their language than any white man had done before me, I never saw one of the nation who could give me either the derivation or definition of the word "Sho-sho-nie." Their country comprises all the regions drained by the head branches of Green and Bear Rivers and the east and Southern head branches of the Snake River. They are kind and hospitable to whites, thankful for favors, indignant at injuries and but little addicted to theft in their large villages. I have seldom heard them accused of inhospitality; on the contrary I have found it to be a general feature of their character to divide the last morsel of food with the hungry stranger, let their means be what it might for obtaining the next meal. The Snakes, and in fact most of the Rocky Mountain Indians, believe in a Supreme Deity who resides in the sun and in infernal deities residing in the moon and stars, but all subject to the supreme control of the one residing in the sun. They believe that the spirits of the departed are permitted to watch over the actions of the living and every warrior is protected by a guiding angel in all his actions so long as he obeys his rules, a violation of which subjects the offender to misfortunes and disasters during the displeasure of the offended deity. Their prophets, judges, or medicine men are supposed to be guided by deities differing from the others, insomuch as he is continually attendant upon the devotee from birth, gradually instituting into his mind the mysteries of his profession, which cannot be transmitted from one mortal to another. The prophet or juggler converses freely with his supernatural director, who guides him up from childhood in his manner of eating, drinking and smoking, particularly the latter, for every prophet has a different mode of handling, filling, lighting and smoking the big pipe—such as profound silence in the circle while the piper is lighting the pipe, turned around three times in the direction of the sun by the next person on the right previous to giving it to him, or smoking with the feet uncovered. Some cannot smoke in the presence of a female or a dog, and a hundred other movements equally vague and superstitious which would be too tedious to mention here. A plurality of wives is very common among the Snakes and the marriage contract is dissolved only by the consent of the husband, after which the wife is at liberty to marry again. Prostitution among the women is very rare and fornication whilst living with the husband is punished with the utmost severity. The women perform all the labor about the lodge except the care of the horses. They are cheerful and affectionate to their husbands and remarkably fond and careful of their children.

The government is a democracy. Deeds of valor promote the chief to the highest points attained, from which he is at any time liable to fall for misdemeanor in office. Their population amounts to between 5,000 and 6,000, about half of which live in large villages and range among the buffaloes; the remainder live in small detached companies comprised of from two to ten families, who subsist upon roots, fish, seeds, and berries. They have but few horses and are much addicted to thieving. From their manner of living they have received the appellation of "Root Diggers." They rove about in the mountains in order to seclude themselves from their warlike enemies, the Blackfeet. Their arrows are pointed with quartz or obsidian, which they dip in poison extracted from the fangs of the rattlesnake and prepared with antelope liver. These they use in hunting and war, and however slight the wound may be that is inflicted by one of them, death is almost inevitable, but the flesh of animals killed by these arrows is not injured for eating. The Snakes who live upon buffalo and live in large villages seldom use poison upon their arrows, either in hunting or war. They are well armed with fusees and well supplied with horses. They seldom stop more than eight or ten days in one place, which prevents the accumulation of filth which is so common among Indians that are stationary. Their lodges are spacious, made of dressed buffalo skins sewed together and set upon eleven or thirteen long smooth poles to each lodge, which are dragged along for that purpose. In the winter of 1842 the principal chief of the Snakes died in an apoplectic fit and on the following year his brother died, but from what disease I could not learn. These being the two principal pillars that upheld the nation, the loss of them was and is to this day deeply deplored. Immediately after the death of the latter the tribe scattered in smaller villages over the country in consequence of having no chief who could control and keep them together. Their ancient warlike spirit seems to be buried with their leaders and they are fast falling into degradation. Without a head the body is of little use.

THE CROW INDIANS

This once formidable tribe once lived on the north side of the Missouri, east of the mouth of the Yellowstone. About the year 1790 they crossed the Missouri and took the region of country which they now inhabit by conquest from the Snakes. It is bounded on the east and south by a low range of mountains called the "Black Hills," on the west by the Wind River mountains, and on the north by the Yellowstone River. The face of the country presents a diversity of rolling hills and valleys and includes several plains admirably adapted for grazing. The whole country abounds with coal and iron in great abundance and signs of lead and copper are not infrequently found, and gypsum exists in immense quarries. Timber is scarce except along the streams and on the mountains. Wild fruit such as cherries, service berries, currants, gooseberries, and plums resembling the pomegranate are abundant. The latter grow on small trees generally six or eight feet high, ranging in color and flavor from the most acute acid to the mildest sweetness. Hops grow spontaneously and in great abundance along the streams.

When the Crows first conquered this country their numbers amounted to about 8,000 persons, but the ravages of war and smallpox combined have reduced their numbers to about 2,000, of which 1,200 are females. They are proud, treacherous, thievish, insolent, and brave when they are possessed with a superior advantage, but when placed in the opposite situation they are equally humble, submissive, and cowardly. Like the other tribes of Indians residing in the Rocky Mountains, they believe in a Supreme Deity who resides in the sun and lesser deities residing in the moon and stars. Their government is a kind of democracy. The chief who can enumerate the greatest number of valiant exploits is unanimously considered the supreme ruler. All the greatest warriors below him and above a certain grade are councillors and take their seats in the council according to their respective ranks—the voice of the lowest rank having but little weight in deciding matters of importance. When a measure is adopted by the council and approved by the head chief it is immediately put in force by the order of the military commander, who is appointed by the council to serve for an indefinite period. A standing company of soldiers is kept up continually for the purpose of maintaining order in the village. The captain can order any young man in the village to serve as a soldier in turn and the council only can increase or diminish the number of soldiers at pleasure. The greatest chiefs cannot violate the orders which the captain receives from the council. No office or station is hereditary, neither does wealth constitute dignity. The greatest chief may fall below the meanest citizen for misdemeanor in office and the lowest citizen may arise to the most exalted station by the performance of valiant deeds. The Crows, both male and female, are tall, well proportioned, handsome featured, with very light copper colored skins. Prostitution of their wives is very common but sexual intercourse between near relatives is strictly prohibited. When a young man is married he never after speaks to his mother-in-law nor the wife to the father-in-law, although they may all live in the same lodge. If the husband wishes to say anything to the mother-in-law, he speaks to the wife, who conveys it to the mother, and in the same way communication is conveyed between the wife and father-in-law. This custom is peculiar to the Crows. They never intermarry with other nations, but a stranger if he wishes can always be accommodated with a wife while he stops with the village but cannot take her from it when he leaves.

Their laws for killing buffalo are rigidly enforced. No person is allowed to hunt buffalo in the vicinity where the village is stationed without first obtaining leave of the council. For the first offense the offender's hunting apparatus are broken and destroyed, for the second his horses are killed and his property destroyed and he beaten with rods, the third is punished by death by shooting. When a decree is given by the council it is published by the head chief, who rides to and fro through the village like a herald and priclaims it aloud to all. They generally kill their meat by surrounding a band of buffaloes, and when once enclosed but few escape. The first person who arrives at a dead buffalo is entitled to onethird of the meat and if the person who killed it is the fourth one on the spot, he only gets the hide and tongue, but in no case can he get more than one-third of the meat if a second and third person appear before it is placed on the horses for packing. A person, whether male or female, poor or rich, gets the second or third division according to the time of arrival, each one knowing what parts they are allowed. This is also a custom peculiar to the Crows which has been handed down from time immemorial.

Their language is clear, distinct and not intermingled with guttural sounds, which renders it remarkably easy for a stranger to learn. It is a high crime for a mother or father to inflict corporal punishment on their male children, and if a warrior is struck by a stranger he is irretrievably disgraced unless he can kill the offender immediately.

Taking prisoners of war is never practiced with the exception of subjugating them to servile employment. Adult males are never returned as prisoners but generally killed on the spot, but young males are taken to the village and trained up in their mode of warfare until they imbibe the Crow customs and language, when they are eligible to the high station their deeds of valor permit. The Crows are remarkably fond of gaudy and glittering ornaments. The eye teeth of the elk are used as a circulating medium and are valued according to their size.

There exists among them many customs similar to those of the ancient Israelites. A woman after being delivered of a male child, cannot approach the lodge of her husband under forty days and for a female fifty is required, and seven days' separation for every natural menses. The distinction between clean and unclean animals bears a great degree of similarity to the Jewish law. They are remarkable for their cleanliness and variety of cooking, which exceeds that of any other tribe in the Rocky Mountains. They seldom use salt, but often season their cooking with herbs of various kinds and flavors.

Sickness is seldom found among them and they naturally live to a great age. There is no possibility of ascertaining the precise age of any mountain Indians, but an inference may be drawn with tolerable correctness from their outward appearance and such indefinite information from their own faint recollection of dates as may be collected by an intimate acquaintance with their habits, customs, traditions and manner of living. I have never known a mountain Indian to be troubled with the toothache or decayed teeth, neither have I ever known a case of insanity except from known and direct causes. I was upon one particular occasion invited to smoke in a circle comprising thirteen aged Crow warriors, the youngest of whom appeared to have seen upwards of 100 winters, and yet they were all in good health and fine spirits. They had long since left the battle ground and council room to younger aspirants of sixty and under. It is really diverting to hear those hoary headed veterans when they are collected together conversing upon the good old times of their forefathers and condemning the fashions of the present age. They have a tradition among them that their most powerful chief who died sometime since, commanded the sun and moon to stand still two days and nights in the valley of Wind River whilst they conquered the Snakes and that they obeyed him. They point out the place where the same chief changed the wild sage of the prairie into a band of antelope when the village was in a starving condition. I have also been shown a spring on the west side of the Big Horn River, below the upper mountain, which they say was once bitter, but through the medicine of this great chief the waters were made sweet.

They have a great aversion to distilled spirits of any kind, terming it the "white man's fool water," and say if a Crow drinks it he ceases to be a Crow and becomes a foolish animal so long as the senses are absorbed by its influence.

Books from Skyhorse Publishing

The Trapper's Bible: The Most Complete Guide to Trapping and Hunting Tips Ever
Edited by *Eustace Hazard Livingston, Jay McCullough* (8.5 x 11, 320 pages, paperback, $14.95)

From the Peace to the Fraser: Newly Discovered North American Hunting and Exploration Journals 1900 to 1930
by *Prentiss N. Gray* (9 x 11, 398 pages, hardcover, $49.95)

Gamemasters of the World: A Chronicle of Sport Hunting and Conservation
by *Chris R. Klineburger* (8 x 9.5, 800 pages, hardcover, $50.00)

Hunting the American West: The Pursuit of Big Game for Life, Profit, and Sport, 1800–1900
by *Richard C. Rattenbury* (12.5 x 9, 416 pages, hardcover, $49.95)

The Lost Classics of Jack O'Connor: Forty Exciting Stories from the Pages of *Outdoor Life*
Edited by Jim Casada (6 x 9, 328 pages, hardcover, $35.00)

Wild Yosemite: Personal Accounts of Adventure, Discovery, and Nature
Edited by *Susan M. Neider* (6 x 9, 224 pages, hardcover, $24.95)